T0215664

Pro PHP 8 MVC

Model View Controller Architecture-Driven Application Development

Second Edition

Christopher Pitt

Apress®

Pro PHP 8 MVC: Model View Controller Architecture-Driven Application Development

Christopher Pitt
Verbena Close 1, Stellenberg, Durbanville, Cape Town, South Africa

ISBN-13 (pbk): 978-1-4842-6956-5
https://doi.org/10.1007/978-1-4842-6957-2

ISBN-13 (electronic): 978-1-4842-6957-2

Managing Director, Apress Media LLC: Welmoed Spahr
Acquisitions Editor: Steve Anglin
Development Editor: Matthew Moodie
Coordinating Editor: Mark Powers

Cover designed by eStudioCalamar

Cover image by Scott Webb on Unsplash (www.unsplash.com)

Distributed to the book trade worldwide by Apress Media, LLC, 1 New York Plaza, New York, NY 10004, U.S.A. Phone 1-800-SPRINGER, fax (201) 348-4505, e-mail orders-ny@springer-sbm.com, or visit www.springeronline.com. Apress Media, LLC is a California LLC and the sole member (owner) is Springer Science + Business Media Finance Inc (SSBM Finance Inc). SSBM Finance Inc is a **Delaware** corporation.

For information on translations, please e-mail booktranslations@springernature.com; for reprint, paperback, or audio rights, please e-mail bookpermissions@springernature.com.

Apress titles may be purchased in bulk for academic, corporate, or promotional use. eBook versions and licenses are also available for most titles. For more information, reference our Print and eBook Bulk Sales web page at http://www.apress.com/bulk-sales.

Any source code or other supplementary material referenced by the author in this book is available to readers on GitHub via the book's product page, located at www.apress.com/9781484269565. For more detailed information, please visit http://www.apress.com/source-code.

Printed on acid-free paper

Thank you, Lizanne, for your patience and support – from the first book to this one.

Table of Contents

About the Author

Christopher Pitt is an experienced PHP and JavaScript/CSS web developer and writer, working at Sanlam Indie. He usually works on application architecture, though sometimes you'll find him building compilers or robots. He is also the author of several web development books and is a contributor to various open source projects such as AdonisJs and Masonite.

About the Technical Reviewer

Matthias Noback is a professional web developer (since 2003). He lives in Zeist, the Netherlands, with his girlfriend, son, and daughter. Matthias has his own web development, training, and consultancy company called Noback's Office. He has a strong focus on backend development and architecture, always looking for better ways to design software.

Before We Start...

So much has happened in the years since I first wrote about this topic. The language has evolved to be useful in more contexts. Package management is a solved problem. Frameworks like Laravel and Symfony are mature and widely used.

When I think back to what PHP development was like, eight or ten years ago, I am amazed by where we find ourselves. It is easier than ever to get started and to make a living building applications using PHP.

Topics We'll Cover

This is a revised edition of the book I wrote in 2012. We're going to cover some of the same topics, but everything has been rewritten from the ground up. Here's a list of things we'll cover:

- Getting PHP set up on our computer

- Writing our first bit of framework code

- Mapping different URLs to different scripts

- Making HTML templates

- Adding validation

- Connecting to the database

- Loading database data into objects

- Testing our code

- Finding and sharing objects in different places

- Laying the foundation for extension

- Adding sessions, cache, filesystems, queues, logging, and mail

- Putting our code on GitHub and Composer

Each new section builds on the same application and prior knowledge, so that more complex topics stay manageable. The previous edition was depressingly academic, and my goal for this edition is to make it as practical and useful as possible.

We'll be using features new to PHP 8 and diving deep into how popular frameworks implement the same features we do.

What Is MVC

A question occurs to me as I begin writing this revision.

Do we still need MVC?

The term was coined in the 1970s by Trygve Reenskaug. It jumped over to web development where frameworks like Django and Rails embraced it.

At the core, it is about separating parts of an application into

- The data and business rules, called the Model

- The presentation, usually of HTML, called the View

- The connecting layer between those two, called the Controller

While it is true that modern web development is a very different environment to where MVC was first thought up, it remains a useful separation of the concerns of an application.

In fact, it's almost impossible not to see these divisions when talking about or building a nontrivial PHP application. As we talk about building modern applications, we'll see bits from many frameworks, and we'll learn what they have to do with this separation.

What Our Focus Will Be

I want us to focus on the core elements of building a web-accessible application in PHP. We'll start with accepting a request from the browser and serving a response.

Everything else should build upon this process.

As we continue, we'll look for ways to add more to this process. As such, I encourage you to follow along with the example application. We'll be building a website for a new space exploration company, called Whoosh.

Whoosh needs a website to sell their space rockets and recruit new astronauts to their cause. We'll start simple, but by the end, Whoosh will have a website that looks great and works well!

Are We Writing Production Code?

We're going to write secure and bug-free code, to the best of our knowledge. While it should be to the level that you can safely use the code we write in production, I don't recommend that you do.

It's probably a topic for another time and place, but there are many benefits to using established, mature PHP frameworks. When you use a mature framework, you automatically benefit from

- Having many eyes on the code, to spot security issues early

- Having many hands to help maintain and upgrade the code

- Being able to hire new folks to work on your applications, who don't then also have to learn your proprietary code to be impactful

Writing your own framework is an excellent way to learn how other frameworks solve similar problems, and it should also be an opportunity to reflect on how much work and pressure popular frameworks can take off your hands.

You get to decide how much of your own code you want to write, but it would be foolish to use 100% of your own code in production.

Ways to Learn PHP

There are many ways to learn PHP. This book will teach things that may be unfamiliar to a new developer, but the goal isn't to be the best place for someone to learn programming (or even PHP) for the first time.

You should be familiar with basic PHP syntax before reading this book. Some topics include

- Using variables, loops, and control flow statements

- Using classes and creating new objects

- Loading different scripts, using require, include, and so on

- Using the command line for common, repeated tasks, like installing new Composer libraries

If you would like to learn programming, here are some resources I'd recommend:

1. Codecademy has an interactive course, where you can enter the code you are learning about and see it work right in the browser.

2. *PHP for the Web* is written by the technical reviewer of this book. It's an excellent introduction to the web aspects of PHP. There's some overlap with this book, but far more detail for someone completely new to PHP there.

3. PHP: The Right Way is a set of best practices, written by experienced developers, to help you avoid common pitfalls in your applications.

CHAPTER 1

Ways to Use PHP

Let's talk about a few different ways to use PHP. The main ones you're likely to encounter are

- Running scripts inside a web server, to make websites
- Running scripts from the command line/terminal

Let's look at a few variations of these. With the exception of coding on the go, I'm not going to go too deep into the setup. By the time you get your hands on this book, instructions like that are likely to be out of date.

You're better off searching for something like "how do I install PHP on [your operating system here]"...

Running Scripts in the Terminal

Have you ever seen a computer hacker in a movie? They are usually hunched in front of a keyboard and screen, typing frantically. Sometimes they are wearing a hoodie.

The truth is that programming and using a terminal are normal things to do. You're probably more used to seeing a terminal window if you use a computer made by Apple or are running Linux than if you are on a Windows machine.

Terminal windows, sometimes called command prompt or console, are just a direct line of communication to the inside of your computer. You can use them to install new programs or run scripts you make yourself.

You don't have to use a terminal window to run your scripts. If you prefer a visual interface, skip ahead.

© Christopher Pitt 2021
C. Pitt, *Pro PHP 8 MVC*, https://doi.org/10.1007/978-1-4842-6957-2_1

The steps to install and use PHP differ depending on the operating system you are using. If you're using macOS, you can use Homebrew to install PHP and a database.

If you're using Linux, you can use a built-in package manager to install the same things.

On Windows, you could try to use the Windows Subsystem for Linux, which will provide the same terminal interface you'd find on a Linux computer. Or you can go with a package manager like Chocolatey.

The official PHP documentation provides an up-to-date list of instructions for how to install PHP on the most common operating systems.

As an aside, the terminal app I use is called HyperTerm. I like it because I can configure it using JavaScript, and I can also use the same theme as I am using in my code editor.

HyperTerm terminal app, running on macOS

Running a Website Through a GUI

Some folks prefer a more visual approach to running their website. There are plenty of good options to choose from, but the one I'd recommend is an app called XAMPP.

You can find downloadable installers for common operating systems, as well as instructions for how to use the installers, on the XAMPP site. As opposed to running PHP scripts in a terminal window, XAMPP will give you a place to put PHP files that are run by a web server. The difference is subtle and important.

When we run scripts directly, they are run until they complete. If they don't complete, it's typically because there's a problem with the script, like an infinite loop.

Some frameworks and libraries introduce the idea of long-running scripts or server scripts. I'm not talking about those in this case. I'm talking about scripts we might want to execute for a simple purpose or that are intended to be run frequently, as part of server maintenance.

Common examples are a script to rename a bunch of files, one to remove old log files, or even a script to run some scheduled tasks.

When we use a web server, the web server takes the particulars of the request (headers, parameters, etc.), and it executes the script. At the end of the day, the same code is run, but the web server is taking some of the work off our hands. It's also taking the output and error logging off our hands, to some extent.

Later, when I ask you to run a script, you may have to interpret that in the context of your web server. If I tell you to run a script, that may mean putting it in a file that the web server can serve. I'll tell you when and what to do...

Running a Website Through a Virtual Computer

Let's say you want to run your code on your own computer, but you don't want it clogging up your filesystem or leading to all sorts of new things being installed. In that case, you can use something like VirtualBox.

VirtualBox is a program you install that allows you to create "virtual computers" that run on your computer. You can decide how many resources they're allowed access to. When they're suspended, they don't use any resources, except the hard drive space they need to remember what they were doing before.

The process of setting them up and using them is not unlike setting up a new physical computer. You need installation files for your preferred operating system, and then you need to install PHP (and other tools) on them as you would if they were a physical computer.

It's a bit more work than installing those on your actual computer, but often a lot cleaner too.

You can use the base VirtualBox application, or you can go a step further and use the automatic setting-up help that comes from a bit of software called Vagrant. It's a tool that lets you use scripts to set up and maintain VirtualBox (and other) virtual computers. You can even use the recipes other people make, so you don't have to do any of the heavy lifting yourself.

I recommend these resources when learning more about Vagrant:

- Vagrant CookBook will explain what Vagrant does and how to use it.

- Phansible will ask what you want installed and then create the Vagrant scripts for you.

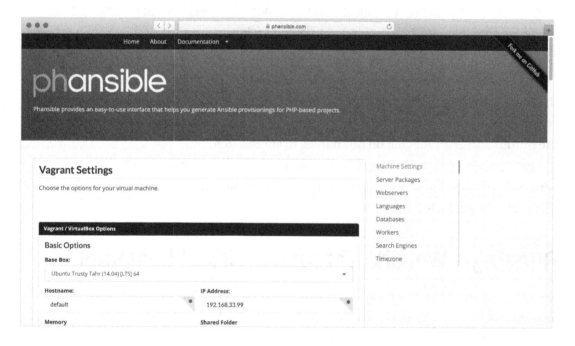

phansible.com Vagrant provisioning tools

Running a Website on a Remote Server

At some point, you're going to want other people to see and use the website you've made. There are ways to allow them to see the website running on your local computer, but they're not meant as a permanent solution.

Instead, many companies offer what they like to refer to as "cloud hosting" or "virtual server hosting." There are some big names, like Amazon Web Services and Google Cloud. There are also smaller names like DigitalOcean and Vultr. I prefer the smaller companies because their management consoles are much easier to understand.

Once you have an account with DigitalOcean, you can log in and create a virtual server. It's similar to a VirtualBox server in that it isn't a physical machine. You can still run popular operating systems on it, like Ubuntu Linux.

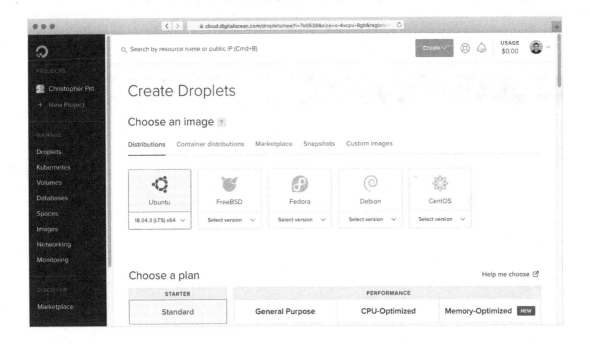

Creating virtual servers on DigitalOcean

In fact, all of the companies I've mentioned will allow you to set up some form of virtual server, running Linux. From that point, you need only follow the instructions you would otherwise have done in a terminal window on your personal computer.

If you prefer someone else doing the heavy lifting for you – as do I – you can use a service like Laravel Forge to install everything you'll need to run a PHP application.

We will be referring back to Laravel often in this book. While Laravel Forge is geared toward supporting Laravel applications, it can host websites built to work with other frameworks and even websites written in other languages.

I host many NodeJS websites on my Forge servers, because I still get all the security and automation that comes from using Forge for those sites.

Taylor Otwell – the creator of Forge – has generously offered a coupon for 35% off the first year of Forge. You can use the coupon code **IHz71w7Z**, added to your billing profile, after adding a payment method (but before subscribing).

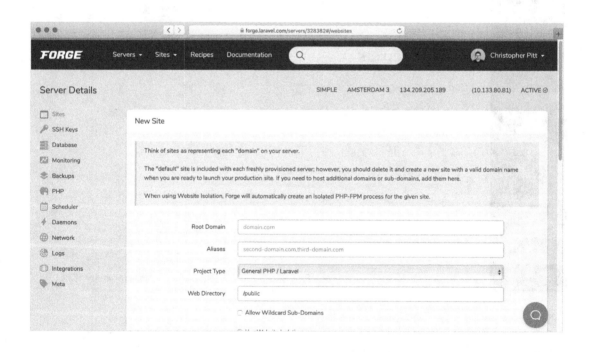

Provisioning virtual servers on Laravel Forge

Hosting "in the cloud" is not free. Some of these companies will give you generous trial accounts, but you'll start to pay for their services sooner or later. Fortunately, you don't need to pay anything to get started with PHP MVC development, so long as you do it on your personal computer...

Coding in a Sandbox

When you want to test out some code, but you're not around a familiar computer, you can code in a sandbox. Sandbox websites allow you to run PHP code and share links so you can demonstrate something to others.

There are two I'd recommend you try:

1.   Laravel Playground is tailored to work well for testing Laravel code, but you can execute any PHP code in it. You can also embed a playground (with custom code) on another site, which makes it great for documenting your PHP code in a wiki or documentation site.

2.   3v4l is the perfect place to see how the same code functions across different versions of PHP. Have a weird bug? Put the code there and share a link to it on Twitter.

Coding on the Go

As a final bit of fun, I'd like to talk about coding on an iPad. A lot of developers I interact with have access to an iPad, but don't really know that it can be a powerful tool for coding on the go.

Here are a few apps I'd recommend you try, if you'd like to explore this topic...

The first app is called DraftCode. It's a PHP code editor that allows for the execution of local PHP code in much the same way as if you were running the code in a GUI like XAMPP. At the time of writing, it costs $4.99.

DraftCode code editor

This is one of the few apps I could find that even attempts to execute code without an Internet connection, which means you can use it on a train or a plane. It has good support for WordPress apps, and I've even gotten it to run Laravel apps in the past.

Unfortunately, it seems the maintainer has decided to offer supported versions of PHP (7.2 and 7.3) as additional in-app purchases. You can use the base app to run PHP 5.6 code, but you'll have to pay an additional $3.99 or $5.99 to unlock the newer versions.

Alternatively, you could try an app called winphp. I haven't had much experience with it, but it appears to offer the same functionality as DraftCode and then some. You can download it for free, but you can also unlock a ton of extra functionality (and hide ads) with a $4.99 in-app purchase.

```
21:07  Mon 01 Jun                                                    100%

<   phpinfo.php   date.php   phpwin.json   index.php

File ▼   Edit ▼   View ▼

 1 <!DOCTYPE html>
 2 <html>
 3
 4   <head>
 5     <title>phpwin</title>
 6     <meta charset="UTF-8">
 7     <meta name="viewport" content="width=device-width, initial-scale=1, maximum-scale=1" />
 8     <link rel="icon" href="assets/img/favicon.png"/>
 9     <link href="assets/css/styles.css" rel="stylesheet" />
10     <script src="assets/js/libraries.js"></script>
11     <script src="assets/js/main.js"></script>
12   </head>
13
14   <body>
15     <img src="assets/img/logo.png" alt="phpwin logo" />
16     <h1>Thank you for choosing phpwin app</h1>
17     <a class="button" href="phpinfo.php">phpinfo</a>
18     <a id="systemDateButton" class="button" href="#">System date (UTC)</a>
19     <div id="systemDate"></div>
20     <div id="footer">© 2020 Firas Moussa | <a href="http://www.phpwin.org">www.phpwin.org</a></div>
21   </body>
22
23 </html>

Ln 1, Col 1, Sel 0 (23 Lines)
```

winphp code editor

Both of these apps support external keyboards and mice/trackpads, provided you can get them to work with your iPad. I find even just having a keyboard cover goes a long way to helping me code. Nobody enjoys tapping a lot of text out on a screen, after all...

Next up, there's an app called Working Copy. It's a Git client that easily integrates with GitHub. The idea is that you'd use Working Copy to clone a repo you're working on and then edit it in an app that can execute code. While you can edit text files in Working Copy, there's no functionality built in to execute those files locally.

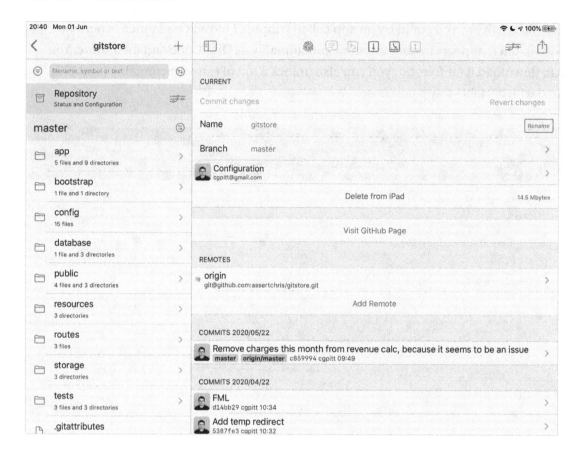

Working Copy Git client

iOS (and, in particular, iPadOS) has come a long way since I first started trying to code on an iPad. Aside from the great new keyboard and trackpad covers Apple has started making, the Files app makes it a lot easier to work with project files.

The last app I want to mention is called Termius. It's an SSH client for iPad. There are many such apps, but Termius is interesting because it has companion apps you can use on desktop, so you can share settings between them.

If you are done with local development, on the iPad, and want to deploy your website to a remote virtual server, you're going to need a way to communicate with that server. SSH is the way. Granted, you'll need Internet access for this part, but if you're used to working on an iPad, then deploying from an iPad might suit you.

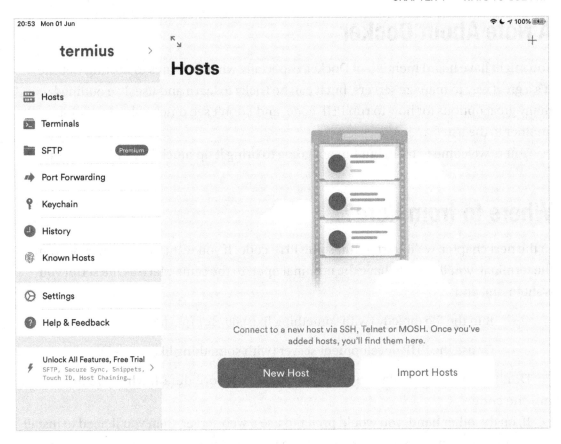

Termius SSH client

As with most of the other apps, in-app purchases will unlock extra features and remove ads. I don't use Termius enough to need those features, so I'm still using a free account at the moment.

Of course, with GitHub offering a code editor built into their app, coding on an iPad is going to become much easier. You'll obviously need Internet access and a paid GitHub account to use that option, but I personally think it'll be worth it for the mobility.

A Note About Docker

You might have heard mention of Docker, especially when it comes to hosting websites. It's a great way to manage servers, but it can be tricky to learn and use. I've outlined many great options for how to run PHP code, and I don't see much value in adding another to the list.

You're welcome to try it, but I'm not going to bring it up much beyond this point.

Where to from Here?

In the next chapter, we'll start to run some PHP code. If you want to run that code from the terminal, you'll need to have the terminal open to the same place as the script you want to run, and

- Run the file directly (with something like `php script.php`).

- Or use the PHP development server (with something like `php -S`).

Don't worry – I'll explain how to use these, in more detail, when we need to run the code.

If, on the other hand, you would prefer to use a web server, then you'll need to install it and put your scripts inside the special "web root" folder. Each web server is different, so you'll need to refer to the documentation for the one that you choose to install.

CHAPTER 2

Writing Our First Bit of Code

It's time to dive in and write some code! Whoosh needs a website, and we're going to build it for them. Since this is the first time we're coding, at least in the context of this book, I'm going to spend a bit of time talking about how and where we write the code.

All the code I show you will be on GitHub. If this is your first time using something like Git, don't stress. It's a system of storing code and tracking changes to that code. Kind of like a database of events that are defined by what has happened to the code of your application. With it, you can go back to any point in your code and see what you had before.

It's also a great way to work with other developers. They can create copies of your code and use those copies to suggest changes for you to make. GitHub provides an easy-to-use interface for reviewing and accepting those changes, so that you always know what's going on in your project.

I'll leave it up to a=the fantastic GitHub guide to Git to cover the basics. There are only a handful of commands you'll need to review the code in this book:

1. `git clone git@github.com:assertchris/pro-php-mvc.git`

2. `cd pro-php-mvc`

3. `git branch -a`

If you're familiar with GitHub and Git, feel free to skip ahead to the part of this chapter where we **handle a request**.

These commands create a local copy of the source code repository in the folder your terminal window is currently in. They then navigate into the folder containing those files and list the available branches in the repository.

© Christopher Pitt 2021
C. Pitt, *Pro PHP 8 MVC*, https://doi.org/10.1007/978-1-4842-6957-2_2

Branches are like different rooms in a house, where each room is loosely based on the previous one. Say I have an application that has three files. I want to add a fourth one, but while I'm working on it, I don't want that file to be in the main branch (or room) of the repository.

I can deviate from the main branch and work on my fourth file in a new branch. I could merge that change back into the main branch, or it could live in its new branch forever. I could deviate, again, either off the main branch or this new one I've made.

This is the pattern I'll use for storing the source code of each chapter. Each branch will have the code of all the previous chapters, but also the code of the chapter the branch is named after. If you're in Chapter 5, you can switch to the branch named chapter-5, and you'll see what the code is like by the end of that chapter.

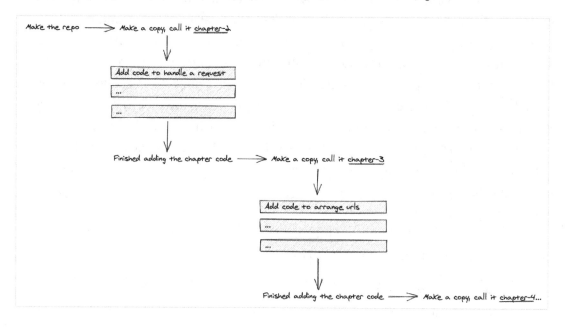

Branching for chapters

To switch to the branch you want to look at, use the command `git switch` `chapter-5`, where `chapter-5` is the name of the branch you want to switch to. If you prefer a more visual interface, GitHub also has a neat app you can try.

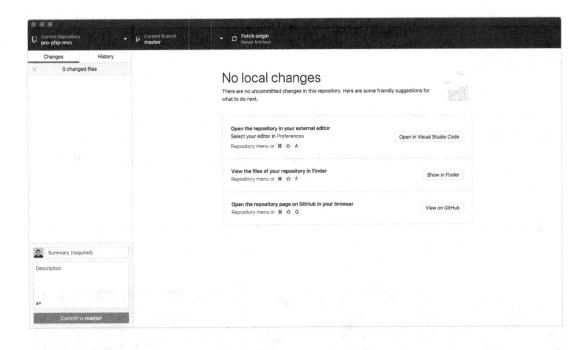

Visually inspecting code from a GitHub repository

If you have trouble finding the code you're looking for, feel free to reach out to me on Twitter.

Handling a Request

The code for this chapter can be found on GitHub. As you've probably gathered, this book is focused on PHP 8, which means you'll need to have that version or you're likely to see error messages pop up. Aside from learning how to make our own framework, we're also learning all the new bits of code we can write in PHP 8…

You can clone the repo to see how I've written things or if you have a pesky error you just can't get past. I recommend you start a separate "new" project, where you write the code you see in this book, as a way of helping you learn and remember.

Open your code editor and create a new project/space for your version of the Whoosh website. My personal favorite is Visual Studio Code, but you can use whatever editor you like.

I mentioned I like to use the same theme in my terminal and code editor. HyperTerm and VS Code both allow a lot of customization. The theme I'm using is from rainglow.io. There, you can find links to instructions on how to install the themes in your code editor and terminal.

Every PHP website begins with a single file. Even the most popular frameworks work this way. Somewhere, deep down, is an index.php file that the web server is sending requests to.

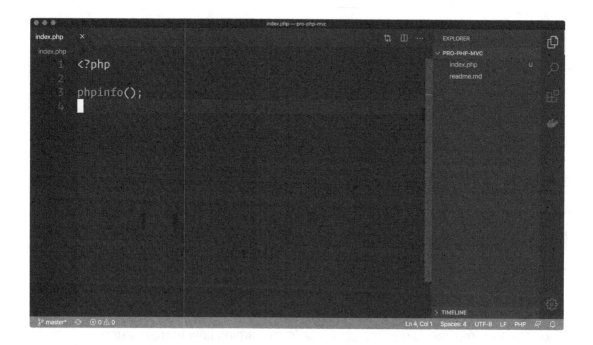

Creating our first framework file

Off the bat, we need to make sure PHP is in a working state. If you're going to run your code through the terminal, you can use a command like php -S 0.0.0.0:8000 from the same folder, and you should then be able to open http://0.0.0.0:8000 in your web browser.

Checking PHP info

Your version numbers may be different to mine, since you're probably reading this a few months after I write it. Regardless, the version of PHP you installed with Homebrew should be the same one that you see on this web page.

If you're running your website through a GUI, a web server, or on an iPad, you'll need to place that `index.php` file in the web root (sometimes just called "root") that the web server is pointing to.

On XAMPP, this means opening the GUI, starting the server, clicking volumes, and clicking mount on `/opt/lampp`. This will mount a network share, which you can open from your code editor.

Whether you run this file through the local development server or through a web server, the outcome should be the same. You're looking for this purplish, grayish page that shows a recent version of PHP.

More specifically, we're seeing a page that shows all the settings and modules that are installed with this version of PHP. Once we know this code is working, we can start to respond to different requests. Each time a PHP script is run in this way, we have access to a bunch of context surrounding the request. Let me show you what I mean:

```
var_dump(getenv('PHP_ENV'), $_SERVER, $_REQUEST);
```

If we replace the phpinfo() function call with a "variable dump," we can see what context is being provided with a normal request.

If it's hard to see all the details, right-click the web page and click "View Source." That will show the underlying HTML that the browser uses to render the page. Sometimes that's formatted slightly better...

Were we to restart the server with a command like export PHP_ENV=prod && php -S 127.0.0.1:8000 and refresh the browser page, we'd see a change in the response.

You may need to export environmental variables differently in your operating system. Later, we'll create a system that works for any machine.

Every framework uses these global variables to determine which bits of functionality it should trigger and which pages it should display. Often, there's a different set of variables depending on the environment the code is running in.

For instance, when the code is running on your home computer, you probably don't want it to access the production database. You'll want to use database credentials that match your home computer.

Different frameworks (and even web servers) have ways of getting these variables into PHP. Some prefer how we exported the variable as we launched the server. Some use specially named files (like .env and .env.production), and they use these different file names to figure out which should be loaded in the current environment.

We'll explore these methods, of loading environment variables, in Chapter 11.

PHP also provides access to variables (or context) about the requests that come through to the script. The variables that are particularly illuminating are those that tell us which request method was used and what path or URL was requested:

```php
$requestMethod = $_SERVER['REQUEST_METHOD'] ?? 'GET';
$requestPath = $_SERVER['REQUEST_URI'] ?? '/';

if ($requestMethod === 'GET' and $requestPath === '/') {
    print 'hello world';
} else {
    print '404 not found';
}
```

If you open http://0.0.0.0:8000 in your browser, you should see the "hello world" message. Changing the address to anything else (like http://0.0.0.0:8000/missing), you should see the "404 not found" message.

We could, of course, fall back to the file-based routing that web servers typically provide, but it's not as useful or specific as this approach. We can tailor responses to match the exact circumstances that should trigger them.

Here, I'm using the and keyword instead of the commonly used && operator. It makes no semantic difference in this situation, but it reads more clearly to me.

Responding with HTML

What can we show in the way of response?

Anything we want, really. Typically, websites return HTML for simple requests. They could also return JSON or XML or downloadable files. We can either return the HTML directly or by way of an include file:

```php
$requestMethod = $_SERVER['REQUEST_METHOD'] ?? 'GET';
$requestPath = $_SERVER['REQUEST_URI'] ?? '/';

if ($requestMethod === 'GET' and $requestPath === '/') {
    print <<<HTML
        <!doctype html>
        <html lang="en">
```

19

```
            <body>
                hello world
            </body>
        </html>
    HTML;
} else {
    include(__DIR__ . '/includes/404.php');
}
```

The kind of multiline string I'm using here is called a Heredoc. They're not new to PHP, but what is new about them is that you can indent them in the way that I am doing here. Until very recently, all but the first line of the Heredoc string needed to be right up against the left-hand side of the file.

The ?? syntax means if the thing on the left is null or undefined, then use the thing on the right.

I've chosen to use single quotes and triple equals. You should know what these mean, if you're familiar with PHP. I think they're good stylistic choices to continue with. If we need interpolation or type coercion, we can use them as exceptions to the general rules of our codebase.

While it's possible to mix PHP code blocks in between HTML, it's highly irregular and can lead to messy codebases. Later, we'll learn how to make our own template engine, which will do just that, but in a way that we don't need to see or work with.

For now, the best would be either to directly output data (HTML, JSON, etc.) or for that output to be included as I have done here. Don't worry about whether this is elegant or not. It's just a first step!

Redirecting to Another URL

Sometimes a successful response doesn't mean a bit of HTML sent to the browser. Sometimes the point is to redirect somewhere else. Say you decided to change a URL from /info to /contact, but you didn't want to break all links to /info that people had already bookmarked.

In that case, you *could* change the URL but maintain what's often called a redirect URL to point to the new URL. That way, when people go to the old URL, they'll be sent to the new one.

This is typically done using a special HTTP header, which browsers should correctly interpret to mean "this page has moved":

```php
$requestMethod = $_SERVER['REQUEST_METHOD'] ?? 'GET';
$requestPath = $_SERVER['REQUEST_URI'] ?? '/';

if ($requestMethod === 'GET' and $requestPath === '/') {
    print <<<HTML
        <!doctype html>
        <html lang="en">
            <body>
                hello world
            </body>
        </html>
    HTML;
} else if ($requestPath === '/old-home') {
    header('Location: /', $replace = true, $code = 301);
    exit;
} else {
    include(__DIR__ . '/includes/404.php');
}
```

With this code, when a user visits the /old-home path, they'll be redirected to the / path. 301 means the browser should remember this as a permanent redirect. You could use 302 if the redirect is only temporary.

[I need to wait for the named arguments roc voting to close before addressing the feedback for this next chapter. PHP might suddenly support named parameters...]

I've written $replace = true, $code = 301. PHP doesn't suddenly support named parameters – it's just a neat way of annotating what those values mean. If I told you the second argument value should be true, you'd have no idea what the value meant without a trip to the docs.

It's assignment, so you should definitely not reuse the names of variables you already have or intend to use. Alternatively, create your own functions that are clear about what their parameters mean or provide good defaults.

Instead of using the header function, we could make our own redirect function:

```php
$requestMethod = $_SERVER['REQUEST_METHOD'] ?? 'GET';
$requestPath = $_SERVER['REQUEST_URI'] ?? '/';

function redirectForeverTo($path) {
    header("Location: {$path}", $replace = true, $code = 301);
    exit;
}

if ($requestMethod === 'GET' and $requestPath === '/') {
    print <<<HTML
        <!doctype html>
        <html lang="en">
            <body>
                hello world
            </body>
        </html>
    HTML;
} else if ($requestPath === '/old-home') {
    redirectForeverTo('/');
} else {
    include(__DIR__ . '/includes/404.php');
}
```

It's also important to terminate script execution (in this case by calling the exit function), because the header function alone doesn't seal the deal. It's still possible to output content after setting it or even replace it with another Location header. When you plan to redirect, make sure it's the last thing you do before the script stops running.

You can also use the die function to terminate script execution.

Showing an Error Page

Believe it or not, we've already handled one common error scenario: when a page can't be found. Really, the only way to know if the user should see a 404 error page is by first checking whether they should see every other page in the site.

But what if the error isn't because the page they're looking for is missing? What if it's something wrong in the codebase?

There are three other common kinds of errors:

1. The URL is right, but the request method is wrong.

2. The URL and request method are right, but there's an error in the code.

3. The URL and request method are right, but there's an error in some other request parameter, like a form input value.

To deal with the first case, we need to keep track of all possible URLs and the request methods that are permitted for them:

```
$routes = [
    'GET' => [
        '/' => fn() => print
            <<<HTML
                <!doctype html>
                <html lang="en">
                    <body>
                        hello world
                    </body>
                </html>
            HTML,
        '/old-home' => fn() => redirectForeverTo('/'),
    ],
    'POST' => [],
    'PATCH' => [],
    'PUT' => [],
    'DELETE' => [],
```

```php
    'HEAD' => [],
    '404' => fn() => include(__DIR__ . '/includes/404.php'),
    '400' => fn() => include(__DIR__ . '/includes/400.php'),
];

// this combines all the paths (for all request methods)
// into a single array, so we can quickly see if a path
// exists in any of them
$paths = array_merge(
    array_keys($routes['GET']),
    array_keys($routes['POST']),
    array_keys($routes['PATCH']),
    array_keys($routes['PUT']),
    array_keys($routes['DELETE']),
    array_keys($routes['HEAD']),
);

if (isset(
    $routes[$requestMethod],
    $routes[$requestMethod][$requestPath],
)) {
    $routes[$requestMethod][$requestPath]();
} else if (in_array($requestPath, $paths)) {
    // the path is defined, but not for this request method;
    // so we show a 400 error (which means "Bad Request")
    $routes['400']();
} else {
    // the path isn't allowed for any request method
    // which probably means they tried a url that the
    // application doesn't support
    $routes['404']();
}
```

There's quite a bit going on here.

Browsers can use different methods for interacting with a web server. For "just reading" website information, they typically send a GET request. For "sending" information to the website (like filling in a form), they typically send a POST method.

It's not super important to understand the mechanics of that right now, but you should be aware that your application will need to handle these different request methods. We'll understand more of how these methods work (and differ) as we start to communicate with the web server in different ways. Chapters 5 and 6 deal with sending different kinds of requests.

Instead of declaring the possible routes inside an ever-expanding if statement, we're defining the routes up front. We aren't defining any routes for POST through HEAD requests, but we probably do want to allow for those request methods anyway.

We also need to generate a list of possible paths, so we can tell if someone is using a correct path (or URL) but the wrong request method. If neither the URL nor the request method is correct, we can fall back to the old "404" behavior.

We can test the 400 error with a command similar to `curl -X POST http://0.0.0.0:8000/`. cURL is a system utility, common in Unix and Linux systems, that can make requests to remote servers. Here, we're asking it to request the home URL, but with a POST request method, which we know should trigger the 400 error.

A fairly recent addition to the PHP language is the ability for us to use trailing commas in function calls, like what I'm doing with the call to `array_merge`. Before 7.4, that trailing comma would cause a fatal error.

Another recent addition is the short closure syntax we're using to define the routes. Short closures implicitly return the values of their expressions, but since we're not using those return values, we can ignore that behavior.

We're also using `throw new Exception` as the single expression of a short closure. That's a new feature of PHP 8.0. The `throw` keyword can now be used anywhere an expression can, which is most useful for short closures that need to throw.

We can take this one step further, by defining an abort method for redirecting to error pages and using it in the event of bad user data or errors in our framework code:

```php
$routes = [
    'GET' => [
        '/' => fn() => print
            <<<HTML
                <!doctype html>
                <html lang="en">
                    <body>
                        hello world
                    </body>
                </html>
            HTML,
        '/old-home' => fn() => redirectForeverTo('/'),
        '/has-server-error' => fn() => throw new Exception(),
        '/has-validation-error' => fn() => abort(400),
    ],
    'POST' => [],
    'PATCH' => [],
    'PUT' => [],
    'DELETE' => [],
    'HEAD' => [],
    '404' => fn() => include(__DIR__ . '/includes/404.php'),
    '400' => fn() => include(__DIR__ . '/includes/400.php'),
    '500' => fn() => include(__DIR__ . '/includes/500.php'),
];

$paths = array_merge(
    array_keys($routes['GET']),
    array_keys($routes['POST']),
    array_keys($routes['PATCH']),
    array_keys($routes['PUT']),
    array_keys($routes['DELETE']),
    array_keys($routes['HEAD']),
);
```

```php
function abort($code) {
    global $routes;
    $routes[$code]();
}

set_error_handler(function() {
    abort(500);
});

set_exception_handler(function() {
    abort(500);
});

if (isset(
    $routes[$requestMethod],
    $routes[$requestMethod][$requestPath],
)) {
    $routes[$requestMethod][$requestPath]();
} else if (in_array($requestPath, $paths)) {
    abort(400);
} else {
    abort(404);
}
```

With the addition of the new code, for handling server and validation errors, we can now respond to all of the most common website errors we're likely to encounter.

It may seem strange, at first, to have the error codes alongside the request methods; but you'll soon start to see (especially in the next chapter) how defining these alongside the request methods is quite convenient...

Calls to set_error_handler and set_exception_handler ensure that our 500 errors are displayed, even if an error occurs that we're not prepared for.

There are two general ways a PHP script can fail. The one is by an exception being thrown. Exceptions are meant to be caught, in a way that can be recovered from.

If an exception isn't caught, then `set_exception_handler` provides a way to be notified about that, aside from the default error message that can be shown in a browser.

Errors, on the other hand, are not usually recoverable. `set_error_handler` is a similar mechanism for being notified. We enable both, so that we can display custom HTML pages for either case.

Setting a custom error handler or exception handler disables the default error headers. This may not be what you want, but you can reenable the headers by adding them back into your abort function:

```php
function abort($code) {
    global $routes;
    header('HTTP/1.1 500 Internal Server Error');
    $routes[$code]();
}
```

Summary

Without really trying, we've made a pretty robust bit of routing code. Routing is actually the topic of our next chapter.

We're going to take all of this code and package it in a class that will remember our routes and decide which one to match and execute, based on the request method and path.

In later chapters, we'll also look at how to improve the templating we started in this chapter.

I'm really pleased with what we've managed to achieve, and I look forward to growing this codebase and our understanding of MVC in PHP 8.

CHAPTER 3

Building a Router

In the last chapter, we put together the code for basic routing. It's time to package this code up in a way that we can reuse and extend.

What Routers Are Used For

Before we can build a good router, we need to try and understand the problem. When PHP first started out, it was common for applications to rely heavily on the file-based routing that web servers offered.

File-based routing is where you have different files for each URL your website responds to. Say you had a `webroot/pages/edit-page.php` file; file-based routing would expose that as `http://your-website.com/pages/edit-page.php`.

In other words, applications were structured (and this reflected in their URLs) to match the layout of the filesystem.

This limits the flexibility you can have when setting up the URLs of your website:

- You can't change a URL without moving files around in the filesystem.

- You can't store part of the URL in a database, like the identifier for a particular blog post or product.

- You're bound by the constraints of the configuration system the web server has, for changing a URL from one form to another.

- As a result, and in larger companies, your ability to change URLs will require the input of another department.

Routing libraries move this responsibility into the codebase, where we can determine what URLs the website has: when and how they respond to requests.

© Christopher Pitt 2021
C. Pitt, *Pro PHP 8 MVC*, https://doi.org/10.1007/978-1-4842-6957-2_3

Some Features We Could Build

I want us to focus on a few core features:

1. Matching request methods and paths to a specific route

2. Handling all the errors we currently do

3. Allowing named parameters in routes

4. Building URLs from named routes and arguments

We already have the basis for points 1 and 2, so the challenge is organizing the existing code in an elegant way. After which, we can look at adding the ability to define required and optional parameters for routes and then reconstructing routes based on a name and set of arguments.

Putting It Together

The more code we write, and the more files we put that code into, the harder it is going to be to find what we want to change. Every popular PHP framework arranges files into folders that group their function or type and for good reason.

When you're working in a codebase that has hundreds, if not thousands, of files, a little bit of structure goes a long way.

I want us to work out a better folder structure for this framework and application. Let's separate framework and application code and load each using namespaces and Composer autoloading:

```json
{
  "name": "whoosh/website",
  "scripts": {
    "serve": "php -S 127.0.0.1:8000 -t public"
  },
  "autoload": {
    "psr-4": {
      "App\\": "app",
      "Framework\\": "framework"
    }
  },
```

```
"config": {
    "process-timeout": 0
  }
}
```

This is from `composer.json`.

After creating this file, we need to run `composer dump-autoload`, so that Composer creates the include files for automatically loading our classes.

Unless we set the `config.process-timeout` property, our Composer scripts will terminate after 300 seconds. A longer timeout, or no timeout at all, benefits us because our development server will continue running as long as we need it to run. Everything we run, using `composer run x`, must obey this timeout.

This means we can put files in app and framework folders and have their namespaces reflect where they are loaded from. Let's start our router by creating a couple classes to reflect the main concepts:

```
namespace Framework\Routing;

class Router
{
    protected array $routes = [];

    public function add(
        string $method,
        string $path,
        callable $handler
    ): Route
    {
        $route = $this->routes[] = new Route(
            $method, $path, $handler
        );
```

```
        return $route;
    }
}
```

This is from `framework/Routing/Router.php`.

The internal `$routes` array stores all the routes we define, using the `addRoute` method. PHP has yet to support typed arrays, but this strongly typed method is a step in the right direction toward knowing what is in that array.

We could also build the `add` method to receive a single instance of `Route`, but that means more work for the folks who will use our framework in the future (who include us).

```php
namespace Framework\Routing;

class Route
{
    protected string $method;
    protected string $path;
    protected $handler;

    public function __construct(
        string $method,
        string $path,
        callable $handler
    )
    {
        $this->method = $method;
        $this->path = $path;
        $this->handler = $handler;
    }
}
```

This is from `framework/Routing/Route.php`.

Instead of how we've been adding routes to a global array, we're going to use a router instance as the object that holds all of our routes. We're using typed properties, which were introduced in PHP 7.4, so that it's clear what types of data our properties are supposed to hold.

Unfortunately, callable isn't a valid type for properties, but we could use `mixed`, which means the same thing as not defining a type. The `mixed` type was added in PHP 8.0. Adding `mixed` doesn't make things better, but we could use `@var callable` so that static analysis tools can at least warn us when they detect problems with variable/property types.

We'll take a look at these sorts of tools in Chapter 9, when we learn more about testing and tooling.

Along with the new `app` and `framework` folders, I also want to use a `public` folder for publicly accessible files, like the initial `index.php` file:

```
require_once __DIR__ . '/../vendor/autoload.php';

$router = new Framework\Routing\Router();

// we expect the routes file to return a callable
// or else this code would break
$routes = require_once __DIR__ . '/../app/routes.php';
$routes($router);

print $router->dispatch();
```

This is from `public/index.php`.

There are a couple things we need to make before this file will run without error. First, we need to make a routes file and populate it with the routes we've made so far:

```
use Framework\Routing\Router;

return function(Router $router) {
    $router->add(
        'GET', '/',
        fn() => 'hello world',
    );

    $router->add(
        'GET', '/old-home',
        fn() => $router->redirect('/'),
    );

    $router->add(
        'GET', '/has-server-error',
        fn() => throw new Exception(),
    );

    $router->add(
        'GET', '/has-validation-error',
        fn() => $router->dispatchNotAllowed(),
    );
};
```

This is from app/routes.php.

PHP include files can return anything, including closures, which is actually a neat way of packaging code that would otherwise require global variables or service location to use.

Service location is a whole other can of worms. We're going to learn more about it in Chapter 10.

We often see returned arrays for configuration, but seldom returned closures, at least when it comes to popular frameworks...

We also need to add a dispatch method to the router:

```php
public function dispatch()
{
    $paths = $this->paths();

    $requestMethod = $_SERVER['REQUEST_METHOD'] ?? 'GET';
    $requestPath = $_SERVER['REQUEST_URI'] ?? '/';

    // this looks through the defined routes and returns
    // the first that matches the requested method and path
    $matching = $this->match($requestMethod, $requestPath);

    if ($matching) {
        try {
            // this action could throw and exception
            // so we catch it and display the global error
            // page that we will define in the routes file
            return $matching->dispatch();
        }
        catch (Throwable $e) {
            return $this->dispatchError();
        }
    }

    // if the path is defined for a different method
    // we can show a unique error page for it
    if (in_array($requestPath, $paths)) {
        return $this->dispatchNotAllowed();
    }

    return $this->dispatchNotFound();
}
```

```php
private function paths(): array
{
    $paths = [];

    foreach ($this->routes as $route) {
        $paths[] = $route->path();
    }

    return $paths;
}

private function match(string $method, string $path): ?Route
{
    foreach ($this->routes as $route) {
        if ($route->matches($method, $path)) {
            return $route;
        }
    }

    return null;
}
```

This is from `framework/Routing/Router.php`.

The dispatch method is similar to the imperative code we had, previously, in `index.php`. We get a list of all possible paths, regardless of their method.

One thing we're doing differently is allowing the Route objects to tell us if they match a method and path or not. Here's what that method looks like:

```php
public function method(string $method): string
{
    return $this->method;
}

public function path(string $path): string
{
    return $this->path;
}
```

```php
public function matches(string $method, string $path): bool
{
    return $this->method === $method
        && $this->path === $path;
}

public function dispatch()
{
    return call_user_func($this->handler);
}
```

This is from `framework/Routing/Route.php`.

This is an interesting, and sometimes contentious, way of defining getters. Some prefer more explicit setter and getter names, like getPath and setPath, instead.

I don't feel strongly either way, but it's important to pick an approach and stick to it throughout. The router's dispatch method also mentions individual methods to handle each error case:

```php
protected array $errorHandler = [];

public function errorHandler(int $code, callable $handler)
{
    $this->errorHandlers[$code] = $handler;
}

public function dispatchNotAllowed()
{
    $this->errorHandlers[400] ??= fn() => "not allowed";
    return $this->errorHandlers[400]();
}

public function dispatchNotFound()
{
    $this->errorHandlers[404] ??= fn() => "not found";
    return $this->errorHandlers[404]();
}
```

```
public function dispatchError()
{
    $this->errorHandlers[500] ??= fn() => "server error";
    return $this->errorHandlers[500]();
}
public function redirect($path)
{
    header(
        "Location: {$path}", $replace = true, $code = 301
    );
    exit;
}
```

This is from `framework/Routing/Router.php`.

The ??=, or null coalescing assignment operator, is similar to the ?? operator we learned about last chapter. It says that the left-hand side should be set equal to the right-hand side if the left-hand side is null or undefined.

This not only allows us to define custom "routes" for error states but creates a set of defaults that are useful without any configuration. We could override the error handler for the 404 page, for example:

```
$router->errorHandler(404, fn() => 'whoops!');
```

This is from `app/routes.php`.

Adding Named Route Parameters to the Mix

We've got a decent set of functionality, for handling all the types of URLs and methods we were handling last chapter. Now, it's time to take things up a notch.

It's common for web applications to respond to URLs built with dynamic data. When you go to a social media site and click a profile picture, you may expect to be taken to a public profile page for that user – something that has their unique name in the URL.

My Twitter profile, for instance, has the URL `https://twitter.com/assertchris`. `assertchris` is the dynamic portion of the URL, because it is different for other users.

Different frameworks call this kind of URL segment different things, but we'll settle for calling it a named route parameter. "Named" because we want to get at that data inside our application, and we do that by referring to its name.

We're going to start with a simple implementation of named route parameters and improve it as the Whoosh website needs to grow. Our named route parameters will come in two flavors:

- /products/{product}: Where the router expects a value to be given for product

- /services/{service?}: Where the router will accept a value for service, but it is optional and the URL should still work without it

---

Most routers allow pattern matching for named route parameters, using regular expressions or a DSL; our router will allow any non-forward-slash character. Consider it a fun challenge to extend the code we write to handle patterns.

Here's an example of how we might define and handle these routes:

```
$router->add(
    'GET', '/products/view/{product}',
    function () use ($router) {
        $parameters = $router->current()->parameters();
        return "product is {$parameters['product']}";
    },
);

$router->add(
    'GET', '/services/view/{service?}',
    function () use ($router) {
        $parameters = $router->current()->parameters();

        if (empty($parameters['service'])) {
            return 'all services';
        }

        return "service is {$parameters['service']}";
    },
);
```

This is from `app/routes.php`.

Assuming we are in the handler for a matched route (I'm going to start calling these actions), we should be able to access details about the current route. Some of those details may be the named route parameters that were matched along with the route.

This means we need to define a new property and method in our `Router`:

```
protected Route $current;

public function current(): ?Route
{
    return $this->current;
}
```

This is from `framework/Routing/Router.php`.

This follows the same naming scheme as our other getters and setters, only we're restricting how the current route can be set. It makes no sense for something outside to be able to choose the current route.

The route matching code changes quite a bit:

```
protected array $parameters = [];

public function parameters(): array
{
    return $this->parameters;
}

public function matches(string $method, string $path): bool
{
    // if there's a literal match then don't waste
    // any more time trying to match with
    // a regular expression
    if (
        $this->method === $method
        && $this->path === $path
```

```php
) {
    return true;
}

$parameterNames = [];

// the normalisePath method ensures there's a '/'
// before and after the path, while also
// removing duplicate '/' characters
//
// examples:
// → '' becomes '/'
// → 'home' becomes '/home/'
// → 'product/{id}' becomes '/product/{id}/'
$pattern = $this->normalisePath($this->path);

// get all the parameter names and replace them with
// regular expression syntax, to match optional or
// required parameters
//
// examples:
// → '/home/' remains '/home/'
// → '/product/{id}/' becomes '/product/([^/]+)/'
// → '/blog/{slug?}/' becomes '/blog/([^/]*)(?:/?)'
$pattern = preg_replace_callback(
    '#{([^}]+)}/#',
    function (array $found) use (&$parameterNames) {
        array_push(
            $parameterNames, rtrim($found[1], '?')
        );

        // if it's an optional parameter, we make the
        // following slash optional as well
        if (str_ends_with($found[1], '?')) {
            return '([^/]*)(?:/?)';
        }
```

```php
            return '([^/]+)/';
        },
        $pattern,
    );

    // if there are no route parameters, and it
    // wasn't a literal match, then this route
    // will never match the requested path
    if (
        !str_contains($pattern, '+')
        && !str_contains($pattern, '*')
    ) {
        return false;
    }

    preg_match_all(
        "#{$pattern}#", $this->normalisePath($path), $matches
    );

    $parameterValues = [];

    if (count($matches[1]) > 0) {
        // if the route matches the request path then
        // we need to assemble the parameters before
        // we can return true for the match
        foreach ($matches[1] as $value) {
            array_push($parameterValues, $value);
        }

        // make an empty array so that we can still
        // call array_combine with optional parameters
        // which may not have been provided
        $emptyValues = array_fill(
            0, count($parameterNames), null
        );
```

```
        // += syntax for arrays means: take values from the
        // right-hand side and only add them to the left-hand
        // side if the same key doesn't already exist.
        //
        // you'll usually want to use array_merge to combine
        // arrays, but this is an interesting use for +=
        $parameterValues += $emptyValues;

        $this->parameters = array_combine(
            $parameterNames,
            $parameterValues,
        );

        return true;
    }

    return false;
}

private function normalisePath(string $path): string
{
    $path = trim($path, '/');
    $path = "/{$path}/";

    // remove multiple '/' in a row
    $path = preg_replace('/[\/]{2,}/', '/', $path);

    return $path;
}
```

This is from framework/Routing/Route.php.

The Route class still supports the literal matching we had previously. If there is a literal match (e.g., '/home/' === '/home/'), then we don't waste any more time trying to match a regular expression.

We've added a normalisePath path method to add a single / to the beginning and end of the path. This makes paths like '' work because they become '/'. The normalisePath method also makes sure that there aren't multiple / characters in a row.

We're always trying to match a known path – the one we find in the $_REQUEST global array – with an unknown set of routes. We can use the following rules to figure out if we're dealing with a possible match:

1. If the route has a simple path (like home) and we have a string match to the request path, then the route is a match.

2. If the route doesn't have any parameters (that bit where we're checking for * or ? in the route path), then it can't be a match. Remember that we know it wasn't a literal match if it reaches this point.

3. If the route path pattern matches the request path (after the names have been replaced with nameless regular expression bits), then we can assume it's a match.

We can use the str_ends_with function, added in PHP 8.0, because it's much simpler than any alternative methods for finding the last character.

Let's look at a couple examples:

1. We can define a route with the path products/{id}/view.

2. A request is made to products/1/view.

3. Since products/{id}/view is not a literal match to products/1/view, we don't exit match early.

4. normalisePath turns products/{id}/view into /products/{id}/view/, and preg_replace_callback then turns it into /products/([^/]+)/view/.

5. preg_match_all sees this as a match for /products/1/view/.

6. The id parameter is assigned a value of '1', and the match function returns true.

And for optional parameters...

1. We can define a route with a path of blog/{slug?}.

2. A request is made to blog/hello-world.

3. `normalisePath` turns blog/{slug?} into /blog/{slug?}/, and `preg_replace_callback` then turns it into /blog/([^/]*)(?:/?).

4. `preg_match_all` sees this as a match for /blog/hello-world/.

5. The `slug` parameter is assigned a value of `'hello-world'`, and the `match` function returns `true`.

6. A request to /blog/ would also match, but the `slug` parameter would then contain a value of `null`.

Building URLs from Named Routes

When working on a large application, it's often useful to refer to other parts of the application by name. This is especially true when we need to show URLs to our users.

Imagine we're building a page that lists the products Whoosh sells. If we had too many to fit on one page, we might want to have links to next and previous pages.

We could hard-code those URLs (while still having dynamic values for what those previous and next pages are supposed to be), but it would be a lot of repeated code and would add to the number of places we'd need to change if we wanted to change the URL.

Duplicate code isn't always bad. It's not the only reason you should use named routes, but it is a nice benefit of having named routes.

The named route might look something like this:

```php
$router->add(
    'GET', '/products/{page?}',
    function () use ($router) {
        $parameters = $router->current()->parameters();
        $parameters['page'] ??= 1;

        return "products for page {$parameters['page']}";
    },
)->name('product-list');
```

This is from app/`routes.php`.

It would be convenient if we could request the URL for this route with the following code:

```
$router->route('product-list', ['page' => 2])
```

We'd have to add some code to the Router:

```
use Exception;

// ...later

public function route(
    string $name,
    array $parameters = [],
): string
{
    foreach ($this->routes as $route) {
        if ($route->name() === $name) {
            $finds = [];
            $replaces = [];

            foreach ($parameters as $key => $value) {
                // one set for required parameters
                array_push($finds, "{{$key}}");
                array_push($replaces, $value);

                // ...and another for optional parameters
                array_push($finds, "{{$key}?}");
                array_push($replaces, $value);
            }

            $path = $route->path();
            $path = str_replace($finds, $replaces, $path);

            // remove any optional parameters not provided
            $path = preg_replace('#{[^}]+}#', '', $path);

            // we should think about warning if a required
            // parameter hasn't been provided...
```

```
            return $path;
        }
    }

    throw new Exception('no route with that name');
}
```

This is from framework/Routing/Router.php.

We can use the str_replace function to swap out all the named route parameters (optional and required) with the corresponding parameters provided to this new route method.

If no route has the same name, we can throw an exception to let the user know. Our usual exception handling will kick in, but we're going to experiment with more useful ways of showing exceptions in the next chapter.

We still need to add that name method to our Route class:

```
protected ?string $name = null;

public function name(string $name = null): mixed
{
    if ($name) {
        $this->name = $name;
        return $this;
    }

    return $this->name;
}
```

This is from framework/Routing/Route.php.

I feel like the route method we've added to Router could also live in the Route class, but it doesn't make a huge difference to me. Regardless, this gives us a way to making URLs by just knowing the route name and providing any required parameters needed to construct the route.

How the Experts Do It

Understanding the problem and how we solve it is only part of what it takes to build a balanced routing library. We're going to take a look at a couple popular routing libraries.

Going forward, we'll review popular open source alternatives to the parts of our framework that we build. This is essential for learning about the edge cases in our code and the features we need or could do without.

The Symfony Router

Symfony is a popular MVC framework, with components used by many other frameworks and projects. Symfony has a great router, so let's look at the functionality it provides.

Symfony provides a similar PHP configuration to the one we came up with:

```
use App\Controller\BlogController;
use Symfony\Component\Routing\Loader\Configurator\RoutingConfigurator;

return function (RoutingConfigurator $routes) {
    $routes
        ->add('blog_list', '/blog')
        ->controller([BlogController::class, 'list']);
};
```

They mention controllers (which we'll get to in Chapter 5), but they're similar to the closures we have used thus far. Their add method requires a name as the first parameter, so you can bet they provide methods for building URLs from route names.

They also support annotations as a means for defining routes:

```
namespace App\Controller;

use Symfony\Bundle\FrameworkBundle\Controller\AbstractController;
use Symfony\Component\Routing\Annotation\Route;
```

```php
class BlogController extends AbstractController
{
    /**
     * @Route("/blog", name="blog_list")
     */
    public function list()
    {
        // ...
    }
}
```

There's a bit of extra setup to do before this will work, but it's definitely an alternative to a central routes file. I think it's good for colocating routes and the actions that they are related to.

PHP 8 supports real annotations (as opposed to these comment-based annotations). We haven't added annotation support to our router, but it would be an excellent way for us to learn more about annotations. We'll look more at annotations in Chapter 7, when we build an Object-Relational Mapper (ORM).

Symfony's router also supports named route parameters, with defaults you can define alongside the route:

```php
$routes
    ->add('blog_list', '/blog/{page}')
    ->controller([BlogController::class, 'list'])
    ->defaults(['page' => 1])
    ->requirements(['page' => '\d+']);
```

They allow you to define a pattern that the parameter must adhere to (which takes the place of our catch-all regular expression segments).

Symfony also supports the concept of route priorities. Our router always returns the first route it matches, which can lead to unexpected results. Consider the following definitions:

```
$router->add(
    'GET', '/products/{product}',
    function () use ($router) {
        // ...
    },
)->name('product-view');

$router->add(
    'GET', '/products/{page?}',
    function () use ($router) {
        // ...
    },
)->name('product-list');
```

In that order, even if we were trying to show the list of products, the product view would be matched first. Additionally, we'd probably get an error since the optional parameter for the product list is a page number (not a product identifier).

Symfony's priority system helps to solve this issue because it lets you give a higher priority to routes, so that it can pick the preferred route when more than one can be matched.

The last feature I want to talk about is route groups. Groups are a way to define attributes common to multiple routes. This might be a subdomain that applies to them or a path prefix. Groups are super useful!

There are lots more to learn about Symfony's router. You can check out the official docs at https://symfony.com/doc/current/routing.html and the source code at https://github.com/symfony/routing.

FastRoute

FastRoute is a smaller, stand-alone alternative. I want to dive a bit deeper into how it works, because I think there are some neat tricks it can teach us. At a high level, it supports many of the same features that Symfony's router does:

- Named route parameters

- Parameter pattern matching

- Route groups

Under the surface, it's a very different beast. It allows for custom parser implementations, cache implementations, and even different regular expression matcher implementations (depending on the kind of route being matched, if it's in a group, etc.).

Our router could be a lot faster if we implemented the kind of caching that FastRoute does: where all the regular expression work that our router does is cached to an intermediate format (or file).

We could also speed up the process of creating URLs from named routes if we worked out what the required and optional parameters were as the route was added to cache, instead of as the URL is requested.

Despite all this flexibility, the code to use FastRoute is fairly succinct:

```
$dispatcher = FastRoute\simpleDispatcher(
    function(FastRoute\RouteCollector $collector) {
        $collector->addRoute(
            'GET', '/products/{page:\d+}', 'listProducts'
        );
    }
);

$method = $_SERVER['REQUEST_METHOD'];
$path = $_SERVER['REQUEST_URI'];

// we should remove the query string from the URI
// or the match won't work...
if (false !== $pos = strpos($path, '?')) {
    $path = substr($uri, 0, $pos);
}
```

```
$path = rawurldecode($path);

$result = $dispatcher->dispatch($method, $path);

switch ($result[0]) {
    case FastRoute\Dispatcher::NOT_FOUND:
        // ...show "not found" page
        break;
    case FastRoute\Dispatcher::METHOD_NOT_ALLOWED:
        // ...show "wrong request method" page
        break;
    case FastRoute\Dispatcher::FOUND:
        $handler = $result[1];
        $params = $result[2];
        // ...call $handler with $params
        break;
}
```

This reminds me we need a better way of dealing with query strings in our router. Let's leave that for Chapter 5, when we look at validating different requests to the Whoosh website.

Laravel and Lumen

Laravel is another popular PHP MVC framework. We'll be referring back to it throughout the course of this book. The folks behind Laravel have created an offshoot "micro" framework called Lumen.

I wanted to mention them because Laravel uses Symfony's router, while Lumen uses FastRoute. The developer experience – at least as far as routing goes – is virtually identical in both frameworks.

This goes to show that it's perfectly reasonable to use someone else's libraries (and there are many good reasons to do so) while still making the developer experience your own.

CHAPTER 4

Building a Template Engine

In the last chapter, we spiced up Whoosh's routing, by reorganizing our first bit of routing code into a set of reusable classes and patterns. Now, it's time to turn our attention toward presenting better interfaces.

There are many different approaches to templating. It's a polarizing topic, where disagreements usually come down to where the line is drawn between code that renders HTML and the rest of the code.

I don't want to get into which approach is best, because in the end "which is best?" can usually only be answered by "it depends." Instead, I want to ease you into fantastically intricate approaches, spending a little time talking about what each of them is good for.

What Do Template Engines Do?

I guess we should talk about what template engines do before we look at how to build one. They come in many shapes and sizes. At the highest level, template engines take in snippets of HTML, PHP, or a custom language; and they produce static HTML that will work in any browser.

Basic Variable String Templates

The simplest kind of templates are ones that expect simple variable substitution. They resemble code like this:

```
Welcome to Whoosh! You are visitor number {numberOfVisitors}.
```

53

© Christopher Pitt 2021
C. Pitt, *Pro PHP 8 MVC*, https://doi.org/10.1007/978-1-4842-6957-2_4

We've already seen this kind of templates. Think back to our router, when we added support for named route parameters. Those looked like this:

```
$router->add(
    'GET', '/products/{product}',
    function () use ($router) {
        // ...
    },
)->name('product-view');
```

This kind of template is often used because it's relatively easy to swap variables with their placeholders. Usually, you just need to use the str_replace method.

PHP-in-HTML

PHP started with a far simpler way of writing templates – a way that continues to work in modern PHP:

```
Welcome to Whoosh!
<?php if($numberOfVisitors > 0): ?>
    You are visitor number <?php print $numberOfVisitors; ?>.
<?php endif; ?>
```

This kind of template allows PHP to be used in between normal HTML. It's much more flexible than a basic variable string template because you can use PHP control flow structures to generate complex arrangements of HTML.

Loops are a common requirement in templates, such as in the case of listing all products available for purchase:

```
Products:
<ol>
    <?php foreach($products as $product): ?>
        <li><?php print $product->name; ?></li>
    <?php endforeach; ?>
</ol>
```

Here, I'm demonstrating the alternative forms of if + endif and foreach + endforeach. These are keywords that aren't often used in pure PHP code, but they're exceedingly useful for templates because they convey nesting without curly braces.

Complex Variable String Templates

Given the rigidity of basic variable string templates and the flexibility of PHP-in-HTML, some folks have come up with more advanced string template languages offering more flexibility.

One of the oldest and most popular template libraries is called Smarty:

```
{foreach $foo as $bar}
    <a href="{$product1.href}">{$product1.name}</a>
    <a href="{$product2.href}">{$product2.name}</a>
{foreachelse}
    There are no products.
{/foreach}
```

These are familiar, compared to both basic variable string templates and PHP-in-HTML. Other, newer template engines follow a similar pattern. Laravel has a template language called Blade, which looks like this:

```
@forelse($products as $product)
    <a href="{{ $product1->href }}">{{ $product1->name }}</a>
    <a href="{{ $product2->href }}">{{ $product2->name }}</a>
@empty
    There are no products.
@endforelse
```

These kinds of template engines usually compile the templates you write into PHP-in-HTML, because that's the most efficient way for them to render the resulting HTML.

Complex Compilers

All popular template engines tend to be custom compilers, of one sort or another. Blade is a great example of a template engine that looks simple and works well, but is also doing fairly advanced stuff behind the scenes.

Custom template compilers weigh in at different levels of complexity. The simplest form takes string templates and uses string replacing, and regular expressions, to replace nonstandard PHP or HTML with standard PHP and HTML.

This simple approach is sufficient most of the time, even for things that appear to be HTML superset languages. Let me show you what I mean...

Under the hood, Blade is converting its @if syntax to regular PHP:

```
@if (count($records) === 1)
    I have one record!
@else
    I don't have any records!
@endif
```

...converts to:

```
<?php if(count($records) === 1): ?>
    I have one record!
<?php else: ?>
    I don't have any records!
<?php endif; ?>
```

Recently, Blade added support for a different kind of template syntax. It allows you to define reusable templates as components, which you can include as though they're HTML elements.

Let's say we make a template in the resources/views/components folder, called menu.blade.php:

```
<nav>
  <a href="/">home</a>
</nav>
```

We can use this, in another template, with

```
<x-menu />
```

is rewritten to a lot of PHP code, inside the parent template:

```
<?php if (isset($component)) { $__componentOriginalc254754b9d5db91d5165876
f9d051922ca0066f4 = $component; } ?>
<?php $component = $__env->getContainer()->make(Illuminate\View\
AnonymousComponent::class, ['view' => 'components.menu','data' => []]); ?>
<?php $component->withName('menu'); ?>
<?php if ($component->shouldRender()): ?>
<?php $__env->startComponent($component->resolveView(), $component-
>data()); ?>
<?php $component->withAttributes([]); ?>
<?php if (isset($__
componentOriginalc254754b9d5db91d5165876f9d051922ca0066f4)): ?>
<?php $component = $__
componentOriginalc254754b9d5db91d5165876f9d051922ca0066f4; ?>
<?php unset($__componentOriginalc254754b9d5db91d5165876f9d051922ca0066f4); ?>
<?php endif; ?>
<?php echo $__env->renderComponent(); ?>
<?php endif; ?>
```

This is undeniably horrible code to look at, but it's not meant to be inspected. Blade achieves this by looking for <x-something /> tags and replacing them with a lot of plain PHP code.

It's also possible to nest content inside the component, like you would with regular HTML:

```
<nav>
  <a href="/">home</a>
  {{ $slot }}
</nav>
```

...where $slot is whatever you pass into the element in the template that uses the component:

```
<x-menu>
  <a href="/help">help</a>
</x-menu>
```

If you've done a bunch of JavaScript development recently, you've probably seen another kind of template: HTML-in-JS. It might surprise you to know that this idea originally came from PHP.

Many years ago, a PHP extension called XHP allowed HTML-in-PHP. When PHP 7 arrived, XHP stayed behind. It still lives on in Hack – the Facebook fork of the PHP language.

XHP code looked like this:

```
use namespace Facebook\XHP\Core as x;
use type Facebook\XHP\HTML\{XHPHTMLHelpers, a, form};

final xhp class a_post extends x\element
{
    use XHPHTMLHelpers;

    attribute string href @required;
    attribute string target;

    <<__Override>>
    protected async function renderAsync(): Awaitable<x\node>
    {
        $id = $this->getID();

        $anchor = <a>{$this->getChildren()}</a>;

        $form = (
            <form
                id={$id}
                method="post"
                action={$this->:href}
                target={$this->:target}
                class="postLink">
                {$anchor}
            </form>
        );

        $anchor->setAttribute(
            'onclick',
            'document.getElementById("'.$id.'").submit(); return false;',
        );
```

```
    $anchor->setAttribute('href', '#');

    return $form;
  }
}
```

This comes straight out of the XHP documentation.

Hack provides a bunch of functionality that actually interferes with their example of XHP. The main bit I want you to see is that <a> and <form> are not strings but rather literal HTML-in-Hack.

I want us to build a template engine that (at least) supports naive implementations of all of these. We may not build them to be as fully featured, but we'll certainly learn a thing or two about writing compilers...

Some Features We Could Build

Let's try to get the main parts of each of these types of template engines right and leave the smaller (better understood) details as an exercise for you to do later on. Here are the things I think are important:

- Parsing basic variable string templates

- Composing PHP-in-HTML templates (including partial templates)

- Building a simple compiler, for string and regex replacement of control structures

- Building an advanced compiler, for HTML-in-PHP templates

- Preventing potentially harmful (XSS, cross-site scripting) content from being displayed

Those last two will definitely have holes, but I'll do my best to point them out without overwhelming you. There's a lot to this chapter, so let's get started...

Putting It Together

If we take a look at our app/routes.php file, we'll see the routes we've already defined in our application. The "home page" route returns a plain string, but I'd prefer it to show more HTML. Perhaps something like this:

```html
<!DOCTYPE html>
<html lang="en">
  <head>
    <title>Whoosh!</title>
    <link
      rel="stylesheet"
      href="https://unpkg.com/tailwindcss@^1.0/dist/tailwind.min.css"
    />
    <meta charset="utf-8" />
  </head>
  <body>
    <div class="container mx-auto font-sans">
      <h1 class="text-xl font-semibold">Welcome to Whoosh!</h1>
      <p>Here, you can buy {number} rockets.</p>
    </div>
  </body>
</html>
```

This is from resources/views/home.basic.php.

This is a basic template, and you might be tempted into thinking that's why I gave it the .basic.php extension, but I did that for another reason we'll see in a bit.

The only weird thing I've added is a CDN version of the standard Tailwind stylesheet. This relates to the class names you see further down. I'm going to use Tailwind for most of the styling in the app, because I don't want to spend a minute talking about frontend build chains.

We might imagine being able to use this, in the "home page" route, with code resembling

```
$router->add(
    'GET', '/',
    fn() => view('home', ['number' => 42]),
);
```

This is from `app/routes.php`.

This raises two questions I want us to explore:

1. How do we structure our code so that it's easy to use while being easy to test and refactor later on?

2. Why should we add or omit the `.basic.php` extension?

I believe we can answer both of them at the same time. I want to design a series of classes that will contain the parsing code for all four template engine ideas we want to explore, and our template library can pick the correct template engine class based on the extension.

To put it another way, I think we can choose the template engine to be applied, for each template, based on the extension we give the file:

-   `home.basic.php` would be for a basic variable string template.

-   `home.php` would be for a PHP-in-HTML template.

-   `home.advanced.php` would be for an advanced variable string template.

-   `home.phpx.php` would be for a custom compiler template.

The specific extensions shouldn't matter all that much. It's just a want to tell different kinds of templates apart and reduce the configuration required up front while increasing the flexibility – you can use multiple template engines at the same time without needing to configure the context in code.

I'm following the lead of how Laravel implements extension-based engine selection. It's not the only way to do things, and you should definitely explore alternatives, but I want to focus on how the engines work more than on the different ways to initialize the engines.

Building the Basic Variable String Template Engine

I guess I'm cheating with this subheading, since we're also going to build the structure in which these different engines will live. I want us to work back from our global function, toward a rich set of classes. Let's define a new "helpers" file and autoload it with Composer:

```
use Framework\View;

if (!function_exists('view')) {
    function view(string $template, array $data = []): string
    {
        static $manager;

        if (!$manager) {
            $manager = new View\Manager();

            // let's add a path for our views folder
            // so the manager knows where to look for views
            $manager->addPath(__DIR__ . '/../resources/views');

            // we'll also start adding new engine classes
            // with their expected extensions to be able to pick
            // the appropriate engine for the template
            $manager->addEngine('basic.php', new View\Engine\
            BasicEngine());
        }

        return $manager->render($template, $data);
    }
}
```

This is from `framework/helpers.php`.

Since this function is going in the global scope, it's wise to wrap the `view` function inside a `function_exists` check. I've encountered situations where autoloader files are loaded multiple times, and this function only needs to be loaded once.

We could avoid the `function_exists` check if we were putting this function inside a namespace, but then it would be more difficult to use this function. The trade-off I'm making is that it will be easier to return a new "view" at the cost of muddying up the global namespace.

In Chapter 10, we'll see a much nicer way to "remember" the $manager instance. For now, we can use a static variable, which is just one way to make PHP remember some data between function calls. This code will only create a new manager if the $manager variable is empty, which only happens the first time the view function is called.

We go about adding a reference to where we're going to store our first few views – a path we'll discover how to improve upon later – so that the view engines know where to look for view files.

We also add a reference to our first template engine – the basic variable string template engine. It expects templates that end in `basic.php`. We'll add more engines to the manager as we create them.

You may be wondering why I want us to end all of these files and extensions in `.php`. It's a habit born out of the hazards of allowing people to see PHP source code in files that aren't meant to be rendered as text. You can use whatever extension you prefer, so long as these files aren't directly accessible through the web server.

We tell Composer to autoload this by adding to `composer.json`:

```
"autoload": {
  "psr-4": {
    "App\\": "app",
    "Framework\\": "framework"
  },
  "files": [
    "framework/helpers.php"
  ]
},
```

This is from `composer.json`.

A quick trip to the command line and we should be good to go:

```
composer du
```

---

du is short for dump-autoload. It's the command we use to tell Composer to rebuild the autoload lookup tables.

Now, on to building the two classes we just dreamed up! The first is the manager:

```php
namespace Framework\View;

use Exception;
use Framework\View\Engine\Engine;

class Manager
{
    protected array $paths = [];
    protected array $engines = [];

    public function addPath(string $path): static
    {
        array_push($this->paths, $path);
        return $this;
    }

    public function addEngine(string $extension, Engine $engine): static
    {
        $this->engines[$extension] = $engine;
        return $this;
    }

    public function render(string $template, array $data = []): string
    {
        // render the template...
    }
}
```

This is from framework/View/Manager.php.

As you may have guessed, we store the paths and engines in arrays. I'm not going to bother with methods for removing paths or engines, since I think they're easy enough to come up with on your own.

Similarly, we might want to be able to support multiple extensions for a single engine. We'd have to add another array or change the structure of the existing $engines array, to store multiple extensions for a single engine instance.

If that last task interests you, you may want to check out the SplObjectStorage class. It allows a kind of array-like structure where you can think of objects like "keys." You could use the engine as a key and the file extensions as the value. Another option would be to allow the engine to tell us if it can support an extension, perhaps through an $extension->supports($path) method.

Before we jump into what the render method needs to do, let's look at what the basic variable string template engine class might look like:

```
namespace Framework\View\Engine;

class BasicEngine implements Engine
{
    public function render(string $path, array $data = []): string
    {
        $contents = file_get_contents($path);

        foreach ($data as $key => $value) {
            $contents = str_replace(
                '{'.$key.'}', $value, $contents
            );
        }

        return $contents;
    }
}
```

This is from framework/View/Engine/BasicEngine.php.

The `BasicEngine` takes a path to a file and gets the file contents. For each key + value pair in the provided data, it does string replacements, so that {some_data} is replaced with "hello" given ['some_data' => 'hello'].

I thought it would make the code a little clearer by not interpolating $key – otherwise, folks reading the code might get confused by {{$key}} in the call to str_replace.

The Engine interface ensures each engine has the method `Manager` requires:

```php
namespace Framework\View\Engine;

interface Engine
{
    public function render(string $path, array $data = []): string;
}
```

This is from `framework/View/Engine/Engine.php`.

Now, let's look at how to pick this engine (based on the template extension) and get it to render our "home" template:

```php
public function render(string $template, array $data = []): string
{
    foreach ($this->engines as $extension => $engine) {
        foreach ($this->paths as $path) {
            $file = "{$path}/{$template}.{$extension}";

            if (is_file($file)) {
                return $engine->render($file, $data);
            }
        }
    }

    throw new Exception("Could not render '{$view}'");
}
```

This is from `framework/View/Manager.php`.

Building the PHP-in-HTML Engine

Next up, we're going to build an engine that uses regular PHP inside HTML while adding some useful tools on top. The main tools I want to add are

- Avoiding XSS hazards

- Extending layout templates

- Including partial templates

- Adding a way to extend templates with "macros"

Let's start off by creating and registering the new engine:

```php
namespace Framework\View\Engine;

class PhpEngine implements Engine
{
    protected string $path;

    public function render(string $path, array $data = []): string
    {
        $this->path = $path;

        extract($data);

        ob_start();
        include($this->path);
        $contents = ob_get_contents();
        ob_end_clean();

        return $contents;
    }
}
```

This is from `framework/View/Engine/PhpEngine.php`.

The core mechanics of this engine are (1) extracting the data using the extract function and (2) buffering the output of an include file.

Included scripts have access to variables defined in the same scope. We want to be able to call the view function with additional data; extract takes the keys + values of that array and defines them as variables in the scope of the render method.

We don't need to worry all that much about overriding already defined variables, except for the $path, since the provided $data could define a variable with the same name. It would be confusing if I gave a "path" value to a view and it became a path to the template.

This property is a temporary solution. We'll refactor it away shortly.

We can copy the path value into a temporary property, so that the consumer can define any number of variables without collisions happening.

We need to register this engine inside the helper:

```php
function view(string $template, array $data = []): string
{
    static $manager;

    if (!$manager) {
        $manager = new View\Manager();

        // let's add a path for our views folder
        // so the manager knows where to look for views
        $manager->addPath(__DIR__ . '/../resources/views');

        // we'll also start adding new engine classes
        // with their expected extensions to be able to pick
        // the appropriate engine for the template
        $manager->addEngine('basic.php', new View\Engine\BasicEngine());
        $manager->addEngine('php', new View\Engine\PhpEngine());
    }

    return $manager->render($template, $data);
}
```

This is from framework/helpers.php.

The PHP engine should be registered last, because the `Manager` class returns the first extension match. If your extensions are all unique, then you don't need to worry about this issue. But, if you're using the same extensions I've suggested, then ".php" can be matched before ".basic.php," which would be the wrong template engine to use...

With this in place, we can create a template resembling the following:

```
<h1>Product</h1>
<p>
    This is the product page for <?php print $product; ?>.
</p>
```

This is from `resources/views/products/view.php`.

This view should be loaded through the product view route:

```
$router->add(
    'GET', '/products/view/{product}',
    function () use ($router) {
        $parameters = $router->current()->parameters();

        return view('products/view', [
            'product' => $parameters['product'],
        ]);
    },
);
```

This is from `app/routes.php`.

We're again omitting the extension, and it's selecting and rendering the appropriate template with the PHP-in-HTML engine. Let's hop onto the next bit of functionality I want us to add – avoiding XSS hazards.

XSS (or cross-site scripting) is the name of a vulnerability where users can submit their own content to the site, containing JavaScript, which are then re-rendered in the application.

If I build a comments section on my blog and allow folks to submit their own comments to it, most of the time they'll be bits of text telling me how silly my words are. In some cases, readers might have ulterior motives and submit comments containing script tags.

These script tags could do any number of things, from causing pop-ups to be seen by other users to stealing login session details and sending them to a remote server.

The vulnerability doesn't happen when they submit the script tags, but rather when I blindly re-render their comments out to a place where the script tags can be executed by the browser.

To avoid this issue, we can provide a helper to escape data when it's being re-rendered:

```
protected function escape(string $content): string
{
    return htmlspecialchars($content, ENT_QUOTES);
}
```

This is from `framework/View/Engine/PhpEngine.php`.

htmlspecialchars will convert the angled brackets of HTML tags, so `<script>` becomes `<script>` – which means the script will appear as text. Now, we can re-render scary data without it being evaluated:

```
$router->add(
    'GET', '/products/view/{product}',
    function () use ($router) {
        $parameters = $router->current()->parameters();

        return view('products/view', [
            'product' => $parameters['product'],
            'scary' => '<script>alert("boo!")</script>',
        ]);
    },
);
```

This is from `app/routes.php`.

The helper can be used in the template:

```
<h1>Product</h1>
<p>
    This is the product page for <?php print $parameters['product']; ?>.
    <?php print $this->escape($scary); ?>
</p>
```

This is from `resources/views/products/view.php`.

Don't believe me that the scary data is scary? Remove the escape method call and see what happens. This method of escaping is really popular and for good reason. I would recommend you escape all the time, and the next engine we build will do that by default.

This engine works well, but what about extending layout templates? We don't want to repeat the whole HTML document or repeated bits of code like menus and footers...

We can begin by adding another helper method to PhpEngine:

```
namespace Framework\View\Engine;

class PhpEngine implements Engine
{
    protected string $path;
    protected ?string $layout;
    protected string $contents;

    // ...

    protected function extends(string $template): static
    {
        $this->layout = $template;
        return $this;
    }
}
```

This is from `framework/View/Engine/PhpEngine.php`.

We can use this, to store a reference to the layout template we want to extend, inside our product view template:

```
<?php $this->extends('layouts/products'); ?>
<h1>Product</h1>
<p>
    ...
</p>
```

This is from `resources/views/products/view.php`.

The layout can look similar to the "home" template we created earlier:

```
<!doctype html>
<html lang="en">
    <head>
        <title>Whoosh! Products</title>
        <link rel="stylesheet" href="https://unpkg.com/tailwindcss@^1.0/
        dist/tailwind.min.css" />
        <meta charset="utf-8" />
    </head>
    <body>
        <div class="container mx-auto font-sans">
            <?php print $this->contents; ?>
        </div>
    </body>
</html>
```

This is from `resources/views/layouts/products.php`.

Then, we need to change the render method, to account for using a layout:

```
public function render(string $path, array $data = []): string
{
    $this->path = $path;

    extract($data);
```

```php
ob_start();
include($this->path);
$contents = ob_get_contents();
ob_end_clean();

if ($this->layout) {
    $__layout = $this->layout;

    $this->layout = null;
    $this->contents = $contents;

    $contentsWithLayout = view($__layout, $data);

    return $contentsWithLayout;
}

return $contents;
}
```

This is from `framework/View/Engine/PhpEngine.php`.

This is starting to look a little strange. When building a template engine of moderate complexity, you can approach the rendering process in different ways:

- The templates come in as path strings and return as HTML strings.

- The templates come in as path strings and return as objects **that can be rendered as HTML strings**.

- Templates come in as "template" objects and return as objects that can be rendered as HTML strings.

We've chosen the first approach, because it is the simplest and quickest to build, but it is not without drawbacks. The biggest drawback we can see is that layouts are temporally linked in the engine. In other words, you have to call the extends method inside the template, and the layout name you give is the only layout that can be expressed by a shared engine instance.

Our view function ensures only one manager and one engine instance (of each type) are in memory at once. This means it cannot hold more than one layout property in memory at once, which means you'll only ever be able to use one layout template for each call (or nested call) to the view function.

If we represented the input or output of the PhpEngine as a "view object," then we could store the layout of each template instance in each template instance. We wouldn't need to store $this->layout inside $__layout and clear it. With this implementation, we have to do that, or the server will crash with infinite recursion.

You can see this crash from recursion, by passing $this->layout to view and not immediately setting it to null.

Let's see how we can solve this problem without the gross $__layout variable and how we can allow multiple layouts...

First, we need to create a new "view object" class:

```
namespace Framework\View;

use Framework\View\Engine\Engine;

class View
{
    public function __construct(
        protected Engine $engine,
        public string $path,
        public array $data = [],
    ) {}

    public function __toString()
    {
        return $this->engine->render($this);
    }
}
```

This is from framework/View/View.php.

This is an interesting shift because it means templates will only be rendered to HTML when they are cast to a string – on demand. PHP 8 introduces the ability to set properties directly from the constructor signature. I don't much like it, but it's good to know about. I'm not likely to use this pattern much going forward.

This change to the signature of the render method needs to be rolled out across the engines we have so far. Let's start with the Engine interface and the BasicEngine class:

```
namespace Framework\View\Engine;

use Framework\View\View;

interface Engine
{
    // public function render(string $path, array $data = []): string;
    public function render(View $view): string;
}
```

This is from framework/View/Engine/Engine.php.

I'll leave the replaced lines as comments, so it's easier to understand what's changed. I'll remove these comments before too long, though...

The BasicEngine class also needs a change:

```
namespace Framework\View\Engine;

use Framework\View\View;

class BasicEngine implements Engine
{
    // public function render(string $path, array $data = []): string
    public function render(View $view): string
    {
        // $contents = file_get_contents($path);
        $contents = file_get_contents($view->path);
```

```
    // foreach ($data as $key => $value) {
    foreach ($view->data as $key => $value) {
        $contents = str_replace(
            '{'.$key.'}', $value, $contents
        );
    }

    return $contents;
    }
}
```

This is from framework/View/Engine/BasicEngine.php.

It's not a huge change to how this class works. Mainly, we're getting the data from the view object, instead of the method call signature. This just means we can store information relation to each separate view instance inside that view instance, instead of depending on temporally linked method calls.

The view helper now also needs to return new view instances:

```
use Framework\View;

if (!function_exists('view')) {
    function view(string $template, array $data = []): View\View
    {
        static $manager;

        if (!$manager) {
            // ...
        }

        // return $manager->render($template, $data);
        return $manager->resolve($template, $data);
    }
}
```

This is from framework/helpers.php.

Instead of rendering the templates the moment we call this function, we're going to change `Manager` to return a `View` object:

```
public function resolve(string $template, array $data = []): View
{
    foreach ($this->engines as $extension => $engine) {
        foreach ($this->paths as $path) {
            $file = "{$path}/{$template}.{$extension}";

            if (is_file($file)) {
                return new View($engine, realpath($file), $data);
            }
        }
    }

    throw new Exception("Could not resolve '{$template}'");
}
```

This is from `framework/View/Manager.php`.

With these changes, you should be able to go to the home page, and it should look exactly like it did before. The most interesting bits about this change to how we're handling views happen in the `PhpEngine` class:

```
namespace Framework\View\Engine;

use Framework\View\View;
use function view;

class PhpEngine implements Engine
{
    // protected string $path;
    // protected ?string $layout;
    // protected string $contents;

    protected $layouts = [];
```

```php
// public function render(string $path, array $data = []): string
public function render(View $view): string
{
    // $this->path = $path;

    // extract($data);
    extract($view->data);

    ob_start();
    // include($this->path);
    include($view->path);
    $contents = ob_get_contents();
    ob_end_clean();

    // if ($this->layout) {
    if ($layout = $this->layouts[$view->path] ?? null) {
        // $__layout = $this->layout;

        // $this->layout = null;
        // $view->contents = $contents;

        // $contentsWithLayout = view($__layout, $data);
        $contentsWithLayout = view($layout, array_merge(
            $view->data,
            ['contents' => $contents],
        ));

        return $contentsWithLayout;
    }

    return $contents;
}

protected function escape(string $content): string
{
    return htmlspecialchars($content);
}
```

```
protected function extends(string $template): static
{
    // $this->layout = $template;
    $backtrace = debug_backtrace(DEBUG_BACKTRACE_IGNORE_ARGS, 1);
    $this->layouts[realpath($backtrace[0]['file'])] = $template;
    return $this;
}

protected function includes(string $template, $data = []): void
{
    print view($template, $data);
}
}
```

This is from `framework/View/Engine/PhpEngine.php`.

At a high level, these are the things we've changed:

1. None of the data that we were storing in properties, to render the views, exist outside the View class.

2. When it comes to "registering" the layout for a template, we check for the file that called this method and assign the layout template name to an array of layouts. This is a bit magical, but it allows us to keep calling $this->layout without a slew of other magic storing that layout value in a View object. DEBUG_BACKTRACE_IGNORE_ARGS and 1 are useful for limiting the backtrace to the least amount of information it can contain.

3. When we render a view, we check if there is an existing layout in the PhpEngine->layouts property.

It looks a little less chaotic with the previous code comments removed:

```
namespace Framework\View\Engine;

use Framework\View\View;
use function view;
```

```php
class PhpEngine implements Engine
{
    protected $layouts = [];

    public function render(View $view): string
    {
        extract($view->data);

        ob_start();
        include($view->path);
        $contents = ob_get_contents();
        ob_end_clean();

        if ($layout = $this->layouts[$view->path] ?? null) {
            $contentsWithLayout = view($layout, array_merge(
                $view->data,
                ['contents' => $contents],
            ));

            return $contentsWithLayout;
        }

        return $contents;
    }

    // ...
}
```

This is from `framework/View/Engine/PhpEngine.php`.

Before we move on, let's take a look at this stage-looking bit of code:

```php
if ($layout = $this->layouts[$view->path] ?? null)
```

It's a more succinct way of writing the following:

```php
if (isset($this->layouts[$view->path])) {
    $layout = $this->layouts[$view->path];
```

I'm not sure the optimization is for the better, but I want us to explore varied uses of modern assignment and comparison syntax.

The last feature, of this engine, that I would like to explore is the ability to extend the engine with "macros." Macros are reusable and useful functions that we can access inside the context of a template. We could, for instance, define escape as a macro, instead of as a built-in engine method:

```
use Framework\View;

if (!function_exists('view')) {
    function view(string $template, array $data = []): View\View
    {
        static $manager;

        if (!$manager) {
            // ...

            // how about macros? let's add them here for now
            $manager->addMacro('escape', fn($value) =>
            htmlspecialchars($value));
        }

        return $manager->resolve($template, $data);
    }
}
```

This is from `framework/helpers.php`.

This means we need to add the ability for Manager to store macros:

```
namespace Framework\View;

use Closure;
use Exception;
use Framework\View\Engine\Engine;
use Framework\View\View;
```

```php
class Manager
{
    protected array $paths = [];
    protected array $engines = [];
    protected array $macros = [];

    // ...

    public function addMacro(string $name, Closure $closure): static
    {
        $this->macros[$name] = $closure;
        return $this;
    }

    public function useMacro(string $name, ...$values)
    {
        if (isset($this->macros[$name])) {

            // we bind the closure so that $this
            // inside a macro refers to the view object
            // which means $data and $path can be used
            // and you can get back to the $engine...
            $bound = $this->macros[$name]->bindTo($this);

            return $bound(...$values);
        }

        throw new Exception("Macro isn't defined: '{$name}'");
    }
}
```

This is from `framework/View/Manager.php`.

Since we're going to store the macros in the `Manager`, we will need a way for each engine to get hold of them. How about we add a `setManager` method to the `Engine` interface, so that engines can use that property to get the macros?

```php
namespace Framework\View\Engine;

use Framework\View\Manager;
use Framework\View\View;

interface Engine
{
    // public function render(string $path, array $data = []): string;
    public function render(View $view): string;
    public function setManager(Manager $manager): static;
}
```

This is from `framework/View/Engine/Engine.php`.

We *could* add this method and corresponding property to each engine, or we could use a trait to do the same:

```php
namespace Framework\View\Engine;

use Framework\View\Manager;

trait HasManager
{
    protected Manager $manager;

    public function setManager(Manager $manager): static
    {
        $this->manager = $manager;
        return $this;
    }
}
```

This is from `framework/View/Engine/HasManager.php`.

Then, we need to add this trait into each of our engines:

```
namespace Framework\View\Engine;

use Framework\View\Engine\HasManager;
use Framework\View\View;

class BasicEngine implements Engine
{
    use HasManager;

    // ...
}
```

This is from `framework/View/Engine/BasicEngine.php`.

```
namespace Framework\View\Engine;

use Framework\View\Engine\HasManager;
use Framework\View\View;
use function view;

class PhpEngine implements Engine
{
    use HasManager;

    // ...
}
```

This is from `framework/View/Engine/PhpEngine.php`.

And, finally, we can set the manager instance when we register new engines:

```
public function addEngine(string $extension, Engine $engine): static
{
    $this->engines[$extension] = $engine;
    $this->engines[$extension]->setManager($this);
    return $this;
}
```

This is from `framework/View/Manager.php`.

We can now call `useMacro` – on the `Manager` class – from any engine that needs access to macros. I don't think it's essential for engines like the basic variable string templates, but it is useful for the more complex types.

This might be a good time to create another trait to use macros, but I'm going to leave that as an exercise for you.

We can define a magic method to call `useMacro`:

```
// protected function escape(string $content): string
// {
//       return htmlspecialchars($content);
// }
public function __call(string $name, $values)
{
    return $this->manager->useMacro($name, ...$values);
}
```

This is from `framework/View/Engine/PhpEngine.php`.

This means we can continue to call `$this->escape` from inside the template, and it will use the macro closure instead of a method on the engine.

That wraps up this template engine! Let's move on to the compiler engines. We'll begin with the advanced variable string template engine...

Building the Advanced Variable String Template Engine

The more I think about this name, the more I want to find a better name for it. At the core, it's just a simplified custom compiler that generates PHP-in-HTML templates from a DSL (or domain-specific language).

Earlier, we looked briefly at the kinds of templates that fall within this group. We want to be able to process code like this:

```
@if($hasRocketsToSpare)
    <p>We have rockets for you!</p>
@endif
```

And that should be rewritten to something resembling the following:

```
<?php if($hasRocketsToSpare): ?>
    <p>We have rockets for you!</p>
<?php endif; ?>
```

The good news is that this kind of compiler follows a similar pattern to the PhpEngine class. Let's start by copying that class and stubbing out the extra methods we'll need:

```
namespace Framework\View\Engine;

use Framework\View\Engine\HasManager;
use Framework\View\View;
use function view;

class AdvancedEngine implements Engine
{
    use HasManager;

    protected $layouts = [];

    public function render(View $view): string
    {
        $hash = md5($view->path);
        $folder = __DIR__ . '/../../../storage/framework/views';
        $cached = realpath("{$folder}/{$hash}.php");

        if (!file_exists($hash) || filemtime($view->path) >
        filemtime($hash)) {
            $content = $this->compile(file_get_contents($view->path));
            file_put_contents($cached, $content);
        }

        extract($view->data);
```

```php
        ob_start();
        include($cached);
        $contents = ob_get_contents();
        ob_end_clean();

        if ($layout = $this->layouts[$cached] ?? null) {
            $contentsWithLayout = view($layout, array_merge(
                $view->data,
                ['contents' => $contents],
            ));

            return $contentsWithLayout;
        }

        return $contents;
    }

    protected function compile(string $template): string
    {
        // replace DSL bits with plain PHP...
        return $template;
    }

    protected function extends(string $template): static
    {
        $backtrace = debug_backtrace(DEBUG_BACKTRACE_IGNORE_ARGS, 1);
        $this->layouts[realpath($backtrace[0]['file'])] = $template;
        return $this;
    }

    public function __call(string $name, $values)
    {
        return $this->manager->useMacro($name, ...$values);
    }
}
```

This is from framework/View/Engine/AdvancedEngine.php.

It's mostly the same as the `PhpEngine` class, but we have this mysterious "compile" step, which is where we'll swap out the DSL language with plain PHP-in-HTML syntax.

Let's also register the new engine (and make "includes" a macro):

```php
function view(string $template, array $data = []): View\View
{
    static $manager;

    if (!$manager) {
        $manager = new View\Manager();

        // let's add a path for our views folder
        // so the manager knows where to look for views
        $manager->addPath(__DIR__ . '/../resources/views');

        // we'll also start adding new engine classes
        // with their expected extensions to be able to pick
        // the appropriate engine for the template
        $manager->addEngine('basic.php', new View\Engine\BasicEngine());
        $manager->addEngine('advanced.php', new View\Engine\AdvancedEngine());
        $manager->addEngine('php', new View\Engine\PhpEngine());

        // how about macros? let's add them here for now
        $manager->addMacro('escape', fn($value) =>
        htmlspecialchars($value));
        $manager->addMacro('includes', fn(...$params) => print
        view(...$params));
    }

    return $manager->resolve($template, $data);
}
```

This is from `framework/helpers.php`.

`...$params` is another instance of using the splat operator. To recap, it means that we're taking any number of parameter variables and adding them to an array, so `includes($path, $data)` becomes `$params['path']` and `$params['data']`. The next time we use it, we're unpacking that array into a list of variables again.

Now, when we create a template – with the PHP-in-HTML syntax in and with a new extension – we should see it work like the `PhpEngine` templates work:

```
<?php $this->extends('layouts/products'); ?>
<h1>All Products</h1>
<p>Show all products...</p>
```

This is from `resources/views/products/list.advanced.php`.

Let's make a start on that `compile` method:

```
protected function compile(string $template): string
{
    // replace `@extends` with `$this->extends`
    $template = preg_replace_callback('#@extends\((([^)]+)\)#',
    function($matches) {
        return '<?php $this->extends(' . $matches[1] . '); ?>';
    }, $template);

    return $template;
}
```

This is from `framework/View/Engine/AdvancedEngine.php`.

The first bit of syntax we want to compile is the change from @extends to $this->extends. `preg_replace_callback` is perfect for this because we tell it to return anything between the brackets, so rewriting to the PHP-in-HTML syntax is straightforward.

This means we can shorten our template syntax to

```
@extends('layouts/products')
<h1>All Products</h1>
<p>Show all products...</p>
```

This is from `resources/views/products/list.advanced.php`.

We can follow this same approach to allow control flow statements:

```php
protected function compile(string $template): string
{
    // ...

    // replace `@id` with `if(...):`
    $template = preg_replace_callback('#@if\(((^)]+)\)#',
    function($matches) {
        return '<?php if(' . $matches[1] . '): ?>';
    }, $template);

    // replace `@endif` with `endif`
    $template = preg_replace_callback('#@endif#', function($matches) {
        return '<?php endif; ?>';
    }, $template);

    return $template;
}
```

This is from `framework/View/Engine/AdvancedEngine.php`.

These new bits of syntax allow us to make if statements with less code in our template:

```php
@if($next)
    <a href="<?php print $next; ?>">next</a>
@endif
```

This is from `resources/views/products/list.advanced.php`.

Of course, it would be easier if we didn't need to type that long "print" statement:

```php
protected function compile(string $template): string
{
    // ...

    // replace `{{ ... }}` with `print $this->escape(...)`
    $template = preg_replace_callback('#\{\{((^}]+)\}\}#', function($matches) {
```

```
    return '<?php print $this->escape(' . $matches[1] . '); ?>';
}, $template);

return $template;
}
```

This is from `framework/View/Engine/AdvancedEngine.php`.

This means we can print using this new syntax in our templates:

```
@if($next)
    <a href="{{ $next }}">next</a>
@endif
```

This is from `resources/views/products/list.advanced.php`.

This prints escaped values, but there may be times when we don't want to print escaped values (even though it's not recommended). For this, we can add another "print" syntax:

```
protected function compile(string $template): string
{
    // ...

    // replace `{!! ... !!}` with `print ...`
    $template = preg_replace_callback('#\{!!([^}]+)!!\}#',
    function($matches) {
        return '<?php print ' . $matches[1] . '; ?>';
    }, $template);

    return $template;
}
```

This is from `framework/View/Engine/AdvancedEngine.php`.

So we can now print unescaped values with the {!! ... !!} syntax:

```
@if($next)
    <a href="{!! $next !!}">next</a>
@endif
```

This is from `resources/views/products/list.advanced.php`.

That's all there is to this template engine – adding new regular expressions to handle new bits of syntax. The only other thing we might want to do is allow macros to be called if they aren't defined as existing syntax:

```
protected function compile(string $template): string
{
    // ...

    // replace `@***(...)` with `$this->***(...)`
    $template = preg_replace_callback('#@([^(]+)\((([^)]+)\)#',
    function($matches) {
        return '<?php $this->' . $matches[1] . '(' . $matches[2] . '); ?>';
    }, $template);

    return $template;
}
```

This is from `framework/View/Engine/AdvancedEngine.php`.

Although it's a silly example, we can now include the product details partial template, using the @includes syntax:

```
@includes('includes/product-details', ['name' => 'acme'])
```

This is from `resources/views/products/list.advanced.php`.

It's surprising how much functionality we're able to add, with relatively few lines of new code in the engine. There's a lot more functionality in Blade, but this is a versatile implementation of a subset of its functionality.

Blade also supports that HTML-like syntax, which will require far more complex regular expressions. It's an interesting challenge to add that syntax.

Building the HTML-in-PHP Engine

The final engine I want us to look at, at least partially, is an HTML-in-PHP engine. It's going to require a different approach to how the views are loaded, but I'm sure we can manage.

The first thing we're going to need to understand is the main difference between the previous template engines and this last one. The previous templates have been loaded inside route handlers. What I'm proposing is a kind of template that takes place inside a PHP class:

```php
namespace App\Components;

class ProductComponent
{
    protected string $props;

    public function __construct(array $props)
    {
        $this->props = $props;
    }

    public function render()
    {
        return (
            <a href={$this->props->href}>
                {$this->props->name}
            </a>
        );
    }
}
```

This kind of compiler requires a couple big things to work:

1. Deep integration with Composer's autoloading system

2. A layer that compiles `<a>...</a>` to regular PHP – like `render('a', ...)` – and then produces HTML from that PHP code

I think it would be a bit intense to make the whole thing from scratch, but there is already a custom compiler we could use: `https://github.com/preprocess/pre-phpx`.

Let's talk through the steps it takes, so we can understand how it differs from the compilers and engines we've already built:

- Integrate with Composer's autoloader, so that it can tell when the file that is being included should be compiled. It looks for files that end in a special extension and readies them for the compiler.

- The compiler walks through the source code of these files, matching tokens against regular expressions. It's not the same as the regular expression replacements that happened before, but rather it breaks the string up into a list of tokens.

```
return (
    <a href={$this->props->href}>
        {$this->props->name}
    </a>
);
```

...is broken up into an array of typed tokens:

```
[
    [
        'type' => 'literal',
        'value' => 'return (',
    ],
    [
        'type' => 'tag',
        'value' => 'a',
        'open' => true,
    ],
```

```
[
    'type' => 'attribute',
    'value' => 'href={$this->props->href}',
],
[
    'type' => 'print',
    'value' => '$this->props->name',
],
[
    'type' => 'tag',
    'value' => 'a',
    'close' => true,
],
[
    'type' => 'literal',
    'value' => ');',
],
]
```

This list of tokens is useful because it allows us to arrange the tokens in a hierarchy. This hierarchy resembles

```
[
    [
        'type' => 'literal',
        'value' => 'return (',
    ],
    [
        'type' => 'tag',
        'attributes' => [
            [
                'type' => 'href',
                'value' => '$this->props->href',
            ],
        ],
```

```
        'children' => [
            [
                'type' => 'print',
                'value' => '$this->props->name',
            ],
        ],
    ],
    [
        'type' => 'literal',
        'value' => ');',
    ],
]
```

This hierarchy (or Abstract Syntax Tree) can then be translated into another language or format. In this case, we can replace it with literal plain PHP code for each tag. We can compile the resulting code to

```
return render('a', [
    'href' => $this->props->href,
], [
    $this->props->name,
]);
```

If we're smart about how we manage the components, we can even have them interact with JavaScript in much the same way as libraries like Livewire and Blazor.

I have previously written about how to do that, if you're interested in trying out that approach…

How the Experts Do It

Before we close out, let's talk a bit about what popular template engines and libraries are doing.

Plates

Plates is a library that provides an extensive set of PHP-in-HTML processing. It has similar mechanisms to the extends and includes functionality we added, as well as a set of helpers that do all sorts of useful things – including XSS protection.

The setup is fairly simple:

```php
$templates = new League\Plates\Engine('/path/to/templates');
print $templates->render('profile', ['name' => 'Jonathan']);
```

Then, inside the template they use a familiar syntax:

```php
<?php $this->layout('template') ?>
<h1>User Profile</h1>
<p>Hello, <?= $this->e($name) ?></p>
```

They also support an extension interface for adding custom macros:

```php
use League\Plates\Engine;
use League\Plates\Extension\ExtensionInterface;

class ChangeCase implements ExtensionInterface
{
    public function register(Engine $engine)
    {
        $engine->registerFunction('uppercase', [$this, 'uppercaseString']);
        $engine->registerFunction('lowercase', [$this, 'lowercaseString']);
    }

    public function uppercaseString($var)
    {
        return strtoupper($var);
    }

    public function lowercaseString($var)
    {
        return strtolower($var);
    }
}
```

It's a little more verbose than the way we add macros, but not by much. In general, it's a lovely library to work with, and I highly recommend using it rather than building your own PHP-in-HTML template engine.

You might even consider wrapping Plates inside your own PHP-in-HTML engine, adding your own conventions on top!

Blade

I've referenced Blade a lot and for good reason. It's the golden standard in ease of use, but it works best inside a Laravel application.

It is possible, at least at the time of writing, to use it outside of a Laravel application, but it's pretty tricky to get working in that way.

Aside from the functionality we've already covered, Blade also supports shortcuts for adding custom control structures (if statements, really):

```
Blade::if('cloud', function ($provider) {
    return config('filesystems.default') === $provider;
});
```

This would allow you to use a custom @cloud statement in your templates:

```
@cloud('gcs')
    You're using GCS!
@elsecloud('aws')
    Enjoying AWS?
@endcloud
```

Then, there's the HTML-like syntax I mentioned, which is built on top of PHP classes:

```
namespace App\View\Components;

use Illuminate\View\Component;

class ReceiptComponent extends Component
{
    public $receipts;
```

```
public function __construct()
{
    $this->receipts = auth()->user()->receipts;
}

public function render()
{
    return view('components.receipt');
}
}
```

The components can then be used as

```
<h2>Receipts</h2>
<x-receipt />
```

It's wild! And would take way too much time to cover in great detail. I recommend, instead, that you check out the official documentation for more details about how these components work.

Summary

This chapter has been an amazing journey through the land of template parsing. I've really enjoyed building out all of these examples, and I'm sure there's a template parser in there that you'll like.

In the next chapter, we're going to look at how to build a validation library, and we'll also create a better structure for organizing the code that relates to each route, as well as introduce a better way of showing error messages during development.

CHAPTER 5

Building a Validator

It's time to start adding a bit more structure to our application. We've been very focused on framework code – which isn't a bad thing – but it meant that we've neglected some of the fundamental things we need to start building a proper website.

Most websites have forms. Let's make it easier to build and use them to capture user input! First, we'll need to make an alternative to keeping all of our application code inside the routes file...

What Are Controllers?

We've already covered much of the "View" portion of MVC, and we're going to take a deep dive into the Model portion in the next chapter. In this chapter, we're going to create our first controllers.

There are many ways to organize an application and to separate the run-of-the-mill code from business logic. It's tempting to spend a lot of time on this, but it's not the purpose of this book or chapter. Instead, I'd recommend you take a look at Matthias's book on the subject.

Controllers are defined more by the code they aren't supposed to contain than by the code they are supposed to contain – at least if you ask Twitter or Reddit:

- "Controllers shouldn't contain code that should be shown in the browser, like HTML and CSS."

- "Controllers shouldn't contain the code that deals with the database or the filesystem."

© Christopher Pitt 2021
C. Pitt, *Pro PHP 8 MVC*, https://doi.org/10.1007/978-1-4842-6957-2_5

These suggestions can lead to clearer codebases, but they don't help to explain what code *should* be contained in controllers. Simply put, controllers should be a useful glue between the deeper parts of your application.

In terms of our framework and application, they are where HTTP requests will be sent to and through which responses will be sent back to the browser.

What Does This Have to Do with Building a Validator?

Since controllers handle request data and arrange response data, they are where validation should happen. Here are the main features we'll be building in our validation library:

- Some structure for defining validation functions

- Some prebuilt validation functions

- A way to give simple names to validation classes, so they can be quickly used

- A way to run a set of validation rules against request data

- A way to customize validation error messages

Once we're done, we'll take a look at some popular validation libraries and approaches, so we can get a feel for what's out there.

Improving Error Handling

Before we get started with controllers and validation, I want to tackle a problem I've struggled with since we built our router. In the `Router->dispatch()` method, we're catching exceptions and displaying a simple error page.

I think we can make something more useful, at least for a development environment. Let's install a great open source library that formats error responses:

```
composer require filp/whoops
```

Then, instead of displaying the previous (rather unhelpful) error page, we can show a helpful stack trace:

```php
public function dispatch()
{
    $paths = $this->paths();

    $requestMethod = $_SERVER['REQUEST_METHOD'] ?? 'GET';
    $requestPath = $_SERVER['REQUEST_URI'] ?? '/';

    $matching = $this->match($requestMethod, $requestPath);

    if ($matching) {
        $this->current = $matching;

        try {
            return $matching->dispatch();
        }
        catch (Throwable $e) {
            $whoops = new Run();
            $whoops->pushHandler(new PrettyPageHandler());
            $whoops->register();
            throw $e;

            return $this->dispatchError();
        }
    }

    if (in_array($requestPath, $paths)) {
        return $this->dispatchNotAllowed();
    }

    return $this->dispatchNotFound();
}
```

This is from `framework/Routing/Router.php`.

Now our errors will be easier to track down.

Better error messages

There's a problem, though. It's generally not a good idea to leave something like this up in a production environment, because it could expose secrets that would compromise your server, service, or users.

We need to add something that will ensure this is only displayed in a development environment. We could filter based on the URL, but there's a better solution!

Let's create a file called .env, in which we store the environment name:

```
APP_ENV=dev
```

This is from .env.

It is essential to add this file to .gitignore so that any secrets stored in it don't get committed and pushed to somewhere like GitHub:

```
vendor
.env
```

This is from `.gitignore`.

The idea is this:

- Secrets are kept inside `.env` and things that are environment specific (such as the name or type of the environment).

- `.env` isn't shared or committed to a source control system.

- When the application needs to know one of the secrets or the name or type of the environment, then it looks inside this file.

We can, of course, create a template so that people know what secrets and environment details they need, when they're setting the app up on their machine:

```
APP_ENV=
```

This is from `.env.example`.

It's common to call this file `.env.example`, so that the file name hints toward the file that this is an example of. When you see a project that has this file in, then you can confidently assume that the project will require secrets in a `.env` file.

We've called the environment "dev," but how do we get that value in the router? We can use another great open source library:

```
composer require vlucas/phpdotenv
```

This library reads secrets, in `.env`, and puts them into the PHP environment. We need to "load" these secrets at the beginning of our application lifecycle:

```
require_once __DIR__ . '/../vendor/autoload.php';

$dotenv = Dotenv\Dotenv::createImmutable(__DIR__ . '/..');
$dotenv->load();

$router = new Framework\Routing\Router();

$routes = require_once __DIR__ . '/../app/routes.php';
$routes($router);

print $router->dispatch();
```

This is from `public/index.php`.

The createImmutable method looks for a .env file, so we need to tell it which folder the file is likely to be. Now, we can expect to see our APP_ENV variable inside the router:

```php
public function dispatch()
{
    $paths = $this->paths();

    $requestMethod = $_SERVER['REQUEST_METHOD'] ?? 'GET';
    $requestPath = $_SERVER['REQUEST_URI'] ?? '/';

    $matching = $this->match($requestMethod, $requestPath);

    if ($matching) {
        $this->current = $matching;

        try {
            return $matching->dispatch();
        }
        catch (Throwable $e) {
            if (isset($_ENV['APP_ENV']) && $_ENV['APP_ENV'] === 'dev') {
                $whoops = new Run();
                $whoops->pushHandler(new PrettyPageHandler());
                $whoops->register();
                throw $e;
            }

            return $this->dispatchError();
        }
    }

    if (in_array($requestPath, $paths)) {
        return $this->dispatchNotAllowed();
    }

    return $this->dispatchNotFound();
}
```

This is from `framework/Routing/Router.php`.

With this check, the Whoops stack trace error page will only appear if `APP_ENV=dev`. I recommend that you set the default value of `APP_ENV` to something else, so that folks using your application (or framework) do not see this error page without opting in. It's the safest position to take, as far as security is concerned.

Creating Controllers

Let's move our route closure code into controllers. First up, let's make a new home page controller:

```php
namespace App\Http\Controllers;

class ShowHomeController
{
    public function handle()
    {
        return view('home', ['number' => 42]);
    }
}
```

This is from `app/Http/Controllers/ShowHomePageController.php`.

I like verbose names, like this. There's an interesting discussion to be had about whether or not suffixes like this are good, but here's how I prefer to name common things:

- Models → thing (singular) → "Product"

- Controllers → verb + thing + "Controller" → "ShowProductController"

- Events → thing + verb (past tense) → "ProductCreated"

This naming scheme leads to fewer collisions and confusion, in my experience.

Now, we need to change the route from using an inline closure to using this controller:

```
use App\Http\Controllers\ShowHomePageController;
use Framework\Routing\Router;

return function(Router $router) {
    $router->add(
        'GET', '/',
        [ShowHomePageController::class, 'handle'],
    );

    //...
};
```

This is from `app/routes.php`.

This won't immediately work, for a couple reasons:

- We're already type-hinting `callable` in the `Router` and `Route` classes.

- Even if we weren't, we can't call an array like a function, unless the second item is the name of a method that could be called statically.

Let's fix both of these problems, beginning with the `Router` class, where we remove the type for `$handler`:

```
public function add(string $method, string $path, $handler): Route
{
    $route = $this->routes[] = new Route($method, $path, $handler);
    return $route;
}
```

This is from `framework/Routing/Router.php`.

And now, we can do the same thing in the Route class:

```php
public function __construct(string $method, string $path, $handler)
{
    $this->method = $method;
    $this->path = $path;
    $this->handler = $handler;
}
```

This is from framework/Routing/Route.php.

That's only half the problem. We also need to make the Route->dispatch() method able to handle a nonstatic controller method:

```php
public function dispatch()
{
    if (is_array($this->handler)) {
        [$class, $method] = $this->handler;
        return (new $class)->{$method}();
    }

    return call_user_func($this->handler);
}
```

This is from framework/Routing/Route.php.

This array referencing trick is neat. It lets us split the array into a couple named variables, so we can create a variable class and call a variable method.

The home page is working again! Let's create another controller:

```php
namespace App\Http\Controllers\Products;

class ListProductsController
{
    public function handle()
    {
        $parameters = $router->current()->parameters();
        $parameters['page'] ??= 1;
```

```
    $next = $router->route(
        'list-products', ['page' => $parameters['page'] + 1]
    );

    return view('products/list', [
        'parameters' => $parameters,
        'next' => $next,
    ]);
    }
}
```

This is from app/Http/Controllers/Products/ShowProductsController.php.

This doesn't immediately work, because we no longer have access to a local $router variable. For now, let's change our Route->dispatch method to accept either a class name or an already created object, so that we could potentially provide a controller object that has already been given the router:

```
public function dispatch()
{
    if (is_array($this->handler)) {
        [$class, $method] = $this->handler;

        if (is_string($class)) {
            return (new $class)->{$method}();
        }

        return $class->{$method}();
    }

    return call_user_func($this->handler);
}
```

This is from framework/Routing/Route.php.

We're assuming that if the first item isn't a class name, it's an object. This may not be the case, so you'll probably want to add a bit more validation to this.

110

I'm not that concerned, because we'll come back to this and refactor dependency management in such a way that you won't need or want to pass objects when creating the route in this way.

Now, we can define the route like this:

```
$router->add(
    'GET', '/products/{page?}',
    [new ListProductsController($router), 'handle'],
)->name('list-products');
```

This is from app/routes.php.

We'll need to store the router in our controller, though:

```
namespace App\Http\Controllers\Products;

use Framework\Routing\Router;

class ListProductsController
{
    public function __construct(Router $router)
    {
        $this->router = $router;
    }

    public function handle()
    {
        $parameters = $this->router->current()->parameters();
        $parameters['page'] ??= 1;

        $next = $this->router->route(
            'list-products', [
                'page' => $parameters['page'] + 1,
            ]
        );
```

```
    return view('products/list', [
        'parameters' => $parameters,
        'next' => $next,
    ]);
  }
}
```

This is from app/Http/Controllers/Products/ShowProductsController.php.

The other two controllers we can make are for showing an individual product and showing an individual service. They're small, so I won't show the code. Check out the project repository if you can't figure them out...

The refactored routes file looks like this:

```php
use App\Http\Controllers\ShowHomePageController;
use App\Http\Controllers\Products\ListProductsController;
use App\Http\Controllers\Products\ShowProductController;
use App\Http\Controllers\Services\ShowServiceController;
use App\Http\Controllers\Users\ShowRegisterFormController;
use Framework\Routing\Router;

return function(Router $router) {
    $router->add(
        'GET', '/',
        [ShowHomePageController::class, 'handle'],
    )->name('show-home-page');

    $router->errorHandler(
        404, fn() => 'whoops!'
    );

    $router->add(
        'GET', '/products/view/{product}',
        [new ShowProductController($router), 'handle'],
    )->name('view-product');
```

```
$router->add(
    'GET', '/products/{page?}',
    [new ListProductsController($router), 'handle'],
)->name('list-products');

$router->add(
    'GET', '/services/view/{service?}',
    [new ShowServiceController($router), 'handle'],
)->name('show-service');
};
```

This is from app/routes.php.

This is a lot neater than before, partly because we've removed some debugging routes, but also because it's not littered with inline closures.

I've given names to all of the routes (and arranged existing names so they're consistent with controller names). You'll also see that I've refactored the views so they all use the same layout and engine. You don't have to make these changes, but I recommend them!

Creating a Form

One of the things we need to build for Whoosh is the ability for customers to purchase rockets. They'll need an account, and by extension, the application will need a registration page.

Let's create a form:

```
@extends('layout')
<h1 class="text-xl font-semibold mb-4">Register</h1>
<form
  method="post"
  action="{{ $router->route('show-register-form') }}"
  class="flex flex-col w-full space-y-4"
>
```

```html
<label for="name" class="flex flex-col w-full">
  <span class="flex">Name:</span>
  <input
    id="name"
    name="name"
    type="text"
    class="focus:outline-none focus:border-blue-300 border-b-2 border-
    gray-300"
    placeholder="Alex"
  />
</label>
<label for="email" class="flex flex-col w-full">
  <span class="flex">Email:</span>
  <input
    id="email"
    name="email"
    type="email"
    class="focus:outline-none focus:border-blue-300 border-b-2 border-
    gray-300"
    placeholder="alex.42@gmail.com"
  />
</label>
<label for="password" class="flex flex-col w-full">
  <span class="flex">Password:</span>
  <input
    id="password"
    name="password"
    type="password"
    class="focus:outline-none focus:border-blue-300 border-b-2 border-
    gray-300"
  />
</label>
<button
  type="submit"
```

```
    class="focus:outline-none focus:border-blue-500 focus:bg-blue-400
    border-b-2 border-blue-400 bg-blue-300 p-2"
  >
    Register
  </button>
</form>
```

This is from `resources/views/register.advanced.php`.

Not a lot to talk about here. It's three form fields, inside a form, which submits to a route named `register-user`. For this to work, we need to make a couple new routes, though:

```
$router->add(
    'GET', '/register',
    [new ShowRegisterFormController($router), 'handle'],
)->name('show-register-form');

$router->add(
    'POST', '/register',
    [new RegisterUserController($router), 'handle'],
)->name('register-user');
```

This is from `app/routes.php`.

The first controller is similar to other "read-only" ones we've made before, since it only needs to return a view:

```
namespace App\Http\Controllers\Users;

use Framework\Routing\Router;

class ShowRegisterFormController
{
    protected Router $router;
```

```
    public function __construct(Router $router)
    {
        $this->router = $router;
    }

    public function handle()
    {
        return view('users/register', [
            'router' => $this->router,
        ]);
    }
}
```

This is from app/Http/Controllers/ShowRegisterFormController.php.

The second is where things start to get interesting. We'll need to do the following things in it:

- Get data sent from the form.

- Check if it passes various criteria.

- Return errors if it doesn't pass the criteria.

- Make a new database record.

- Redirect to a success message.

We're going to learn about databases in the next two chapters, so for now we can fake that part. Here's the rest:

```
namespace App\Http\Controllers\Users;

use Framework\Routing\Router;

class RegisterUserController
{
    protected Router $router;
```

```
    public function __construct(Router $router)
    {
        $this->router = $router;
    }

    public function handle()
    {
        $data = validate($_POST, [
            'name' => ['required'],
            'email' => ['required', 'email'],
            'password' => ['required', 'min:10'],
        ]);

        // use $data to create a database record...

        $_SESSION['registered'] = true;

        return redirect($this->router->route('show-home-page'));
    }
}
```

This is from app/Http/Controllers/RegisterUserController.php.

This controller calls for an additional set of functions – validate and redirect. Let's tackle redirect first, since it's going to be the simpler of the two:

```
if (!function_exists('redirect')) {
    function redirect(string $url)
    {
        header("Location: {$url}");
        exit;
    }
}
```

This is from framework/helpers.php.

There are a bunch of different ways to handle redirects, but I think this is the cleanest. We don't technically need to return the result of the call to redirect, but it helps to remind us that redirect is a "terminal" action. Nothing can or should happen, in the controller, after we call redirect.

Setting headers and exiting, in this way, isn't ideal. It would be better for the application to tell the difference between a redirection and a response. We'll build a better solution to this problem when we come to Chapter 9, on testing.

Now we need to work on the validate method. It should create a "validation" service class, to which we can add the available validation methods that our framework supports out the box.

This is what it looks like:

```php
if (!function_exists('validate')) {
    function validate(array $data, array $rules)
    {
        static $manager;

        if (!$manager) {
            $manager = new Validation\Manager();

            // let's add the rules that come with the framework
            $manager->addRule('required', new Validation\Rule\RequiredRule());
            $manager->addRule('email', new Validation\Rule\EmailRule());
            $manager->addRule('min', new Validation\Rule\MinRule());
        }

        return $manager->validate($data, $rules);
    }
}
```

This is from framework/helpers.php.

This is a similar pattern to what we did with the view manager. If this is the first time calling the validate function, then we set up the validation manager.

We add rules to it, like `required` and `min`, so that folks can use those validators in their controllers without needing to add the rules themselves.

Later on we'll learn how to allow others to add their own validation rules into the system, but that'll require a much better structure for "remembering" managers than what we currently have.

Before we dive into the validation manager class, let's look at how the rule classes are defined. They're based on this interface:

```
namespace Framework\Validation\Rule;

interface Rule
{
    public function validate(array $data, string $field, array $params);
    public function getMessage(array $data, string $field, array $params);
}
```

This is from `framework/Validation/Rule/Rule.php`.

Each rule should have a way to tell if the form data passes or fails, as well as a way to return the appropriate error message for failure. Then, we can define each of the rules we're using:

```
namespace Framework\Validation\Rule;

class EmailRule implements Rule
{
    public function validate(array $data, string $field, array $params)
    {
        if (empty($data[$field])) {
            return true;
        }

        return str_contains($data[$field], '@');
    }
```

```php
    public function getMessage(array $data, string $field, array $params)
    {
        return "{$field} should be an email";
    }
}
```

This is from `framework/Validation/Rule/EmailRule.php`.

`EmailRule` shouldn't require there to be any data from the form (since that's the job of `RequiredRule`). That's why we return a successful response if there is no data at all.

On the other hand, if data is present, then we check if it contains an "@" symbol. There are vastly more complex checks that we can do to tell if the value *looks* more like an email address than not, but they do little to ensure that the email address works. And they're a pain to maintain.

If you really care about the user providing a working email address, then send them an email with a link that will verify their account when clicked.

For the `min` rule, we need to check if the length of the provided form value is at least as many characters as the parameter we passed when declaring the validation rule. Remember, we defined the rule as `'password' => ['required', 'min:10']`. This means we need to get the first argument and should check that it is provided before comparing it to the string length of the password:

```php
namespace Framework\Validation\Rule;

use InvalidArgumentException;

class MinRule implements Rule
{
    public function validate(array $data, string $field, array $params)
    {
        if (empty($data[$field])) {
            return true;
        }
```

```
    if (empty($params[0])) {
        throw InvalidArgumentException('specify a min length');
    }

    $length = (int) $params[0];

    strlen($data[$field]) >= $length;
}

public function getMessage(array $data, string $field, array $params)
{
    $length = (int) $params[0];

    return "{$field} should be at least {$length} characters";
}
}
```

This is from framework/Validation/Rule/EmailRule.php.

The MinRule class looks for the length parameter and ensures that the provided data is at least as long. We could probably throw an exception if the parameter is missing, but that should be easy enough to figure out how to do on your own:

```
namespace Framework\Validation\Rule;

class RequiredRule implements Rule
{
    public function validate(array $data, string $field, array $params)
    {
        return !empty($data[$field]);
    }

    public function getMessage(array $data, string $field, array $params)
    {
        return "{$field} is required";
    }
}
```

This is from `framework/Validation/Rule/RequiredRule.php`.

Finally, the RequiredRule class only checks to see that the form field isn't empty.

Ok, those are the rules we need, but how do we make use of them? Here's the validation manager class:

```php
namespace Framework\Validation;

use Framework\Validation\Rule\Rule;
use Framework\Validation\ValidationException;

class Manager
{
    protected array $rules = [];

    public function addRule(string $alias, Rule $rule): static
    {
        $this->rules[$alias] = $rule;
        return $this;
    }

    public function validate(array $data, array $rules): array
    {
        $errors = [];

        foreach ($rules as $field => $rulesForField) {
            foreach ($rulesForField as $rule) {
                $name = $rule;
                $params = [];

                if (str_contains($rule, ':')) {
                    [$name, $params] = explode(':', $rule);
                    $params = explode(',', $params);
                }

                $processor = $this->rules[$name];
```

```
        if (!$processor->validate($data, $field, $params)) {
            if (!isset($errors[$field])) {
                $errors[$field] = [];
            }

            array_push($errors[$field], $processor-
            >getMessage($data, $field, $params));
        }
    }
}

if (count($errors)) {
    $exception = new ValidationException();
    $exception->setErrors($errors);
    throw $exception;
}

return array_intersect_key($data, $rules);
    }
}
```

This is from `framework/Validation/Manager.php`.

There's not a whole lot to explain that isn't clear from reading the code. The `validate` method does the following steps:

1. For each field, loop through the rules.

2. For each rule, get the processor (or `Rule` class) and run the data through its `validate` method.

3. If there's a failure, get the processor's message and add it to the `$errors` array.

4. If there are errors, throw an exception that has a record of them.

5. Alternatively, return the form values that were validated.

Here's another thing we need to come back and refactor. My aim, with this ValidationException approach, is to provide an exception handler that folks can extend/customize, so that they can react differently to validation exceptions if they so choose. We'll come back to this in Chapter 9.

This presupposes a ValidationException class:

```
namespace Framework\Validation;

use InvalidArgumentException;

class ValidationException extends InvalidArgumentException
{
    protected array $errors = [];

    public function setErrors(array $errors): static
    {
        $this->errors = $errors;
        return $this;
    }

    public function getErrors(): array
    {
        return $this->errors;
    }
}
```

This is from framework/Validation/ValidationException.php.

Now, if we submit invalid data, we should see a Whoops stack trace screen. That's not entirely helpful, since we want customers to see what fields they incorrectly submitted.

It would be more helpful to handle validation exceptions at a routing level, so that we can redirect back with the errors:

```php
public function dispatch()
{
    $paths = $this->paths();

    $requestMethod = $_SERVER['REQUEST_METHOD'] ?? 'GET';
    $requestPath = $_SERVER['REQUEST_URI'] ?? '/';

    $matching = $this->match($requestMethod, $requestPath);

    if ($matching) {
        $this->current = $matching;

        try {
            return $matching->dispatch();
        }
        catch (Throwable $e) {
            if ($e instanceof ValidationException) {
                $_SESSION['errors'] = $e->getErrors();
                return redirect($_SERVER['HTTP_REFERER']);
            }

            if (isset($_ENV['APP_ENV']) && $_ENV['APP_ENV'] === 'dev') {
                $whoops = new Run();
                $whoops->pushHandler(new PrettyPageHandler);
                $whoops->register();
                throw $e;
            }

            return $this->dispatchError();
        }
    }

    if (in_array($requestPath, $paths)) {
        return $this->dispatchNotAllowed();
    }

    return $this->dispatchNotFound();
}
```

This is from `framework/Routing/Router.php`.

If the kind of error intercepted is a validation exception, we can store the error messages in the session and redirect back to the previous page from which the form was submitted.

We shouldn't forget to start the session, or else the error messages (and the "registered" session variable from earlier) won't be stored:

```php
require_once __DIR__ . '/../vendor/autoload.php';

session_start();

//...
```

This is from `public/index.php`.

We should also display the error messages, so the customer knows what went wrong. We can do this on the register form:

```php
@extends('layout')
<h1 class="text-xl font-semibold mb-4">Register</h1>
<form
  method="post"
  action="{{ $router->route('register-user') }}"
  class="flex flex-col w-full space-y-4"
>
  @if(isset($_SESSION['errors']))
  <ol class="list-disc text-red-500">
    @foreach($_SESSION['errors'] as $field => $errors) @foreach($errors as
    $error)
    <li>{{ $error }}</li>
    @endforeach @endforeach
  </ol>
  @endif //...
</form>
```

This is from `resources/views/register.advanced.php`.

If there are errors, we can loop over them and print out each one. With a little bit of formatting, we can make them stand out to the customer. And, just like that, we have made reusable form validation!

Protecting Our Forms

I couldn't put this chapter to bed without addressing the issue of Cross-Site Request Forgery (or CSRF). It's a vulnerability that forces a user to do things on websites they're authenticated to, without their knowledge.

Imagine we built a site where customers can buy rockets. Now, imagine someone embeds some JavaScript (using cross-site scripting) on another site that will use our customer's authenticated session to purchase the biggest and best rocket: all without our customer knowing.

CSRF protection makes this much harder, by forcing the authenticated user to initiate the action. This protection depends on the page where the action is initiated generating a unique token and then the page where the form submits to checking to see that the token matches what was expected.

Let's see how this looks in code:

```php
if (!function_exists('csrf')) {
    function csrf()
    {
        $_SESSION['token'] = bin2hex(random_bytes(32));
        return $_SESSION['token'];
    }
}

if (!function_exists('secure')) {
    function secure()
    {
        if (!isset($_POST['csrf']) || !isset($_SESSION['token']) ||
!hash_equals($_SESSION['token'], $_POST['csrf'])) {
```

```
            throw new Exception('CSRF token mismatch');
        }
    }
}
```

This is from `framework/helpers.php`.

The first function creates a token and stores it in the session. The second checks whether the token was provided by a form and whether it matches the session-stored token.

We should secure every consequential controller with this, ideally automatically. As we develop our framework, we'll learn about great patterns we can use – like middleware – for this purpose. For now, we can add the security by hand:

```
public function handle()
{
    secure();

    //...

    return redirect($this->router->route('show-home-page'));
}
```

This is from `app/Http/Controllers/Users/RegisterUserController.php`.

Now, if we submit the form, we should see that exception thrown. We need to add the token as a hidden field:

```
@extends('layout')
<h1 class="text-xl font-semibold mb-4">Register</h1>
<form
  method="post"
  action="{{ $router->route('register-user') }}"
  class="flex flex-col w-full space-y-4"
>
```

```
<input type="hidden" name="csrf" value="{{ csrf() }}" />
//...
</form>
```

This is from `resources/views/register.advanced.php`.

The form should work again, but this time it's more secure.

How the Experts Do It

We've modeled our validation library after many of the patterns that Laravel uses. The framework itself ships with many built-in validators and also has a clear way of extending the validation to add custom validation functions:

```php
namespace App\Rules;

use Illuminate\Contracts\Validation\Rule;

class Uppercase implements Rule
{
    public function passes($attribute, $value)
    {
        return strtoupper($value) === $value;
    }

    public function message()
    {
        return 'The :attribute must be uppercase.';
    }
}

// later...

use App\Rules\Uppercase;

$request->validate([
    'name' => ['required', 'string', new Uppercase],
]);
```

It also accepts closures as validation rules, so you don't even need to step outside of the controller to define your own validation rules:

```
$validator = Validator::make($request->all(), [
    'title' => [
        'required',
        'max:255',
        function ($attribute, $value, $fail) {
            if ($value === 'foo') {
                $fail($attribute.' is invalid.');
            }
        },
    ],
]);
```

This is one of the areas where Laravel makes things super easy for users. As with many of the libraries that make up the framework, the validation library can be used outside of a Laravel application.

Another great validation library is Respect. Here, the rules are defined using a more fluid syntax:

```
use Respect\Validation\Validator as v;

$username = v::alnum()->noWhitespace()->length(1, 15);
$username->validate('assertchris'); // returns true
```

Respect has many built-in rules, so even if you want to use Laravel's validation library, you might find an implement for a validation rule that Respect implements but Laravel doesn't.

Handling Validation Errors

One of the coolest features of Laravel is an extension point for handling any exceptions the framework throws. Each new application comes with an exception Handler class:

```php
namespace App\Exceptions;

use Illuminate\Foundation\Exceptions\Handler as ExceptionHandler;

class Handler extends ExceptionHandler
{
    /**
     * A list of the exception types that are not reported.
     *
     * @var array
     */
    protected $dontReport = [
        //
    ];

    /**
     * A list of the inputs that are never flashed for validation
     * exceptions.
     *
     * @var array
     */
    protected $dontFlash = [
        'password',
        'password_confirmation',
    ];

    /**
     * Register the exception handling callbacks for the application.
     *
     * @return void
     */
    public function register()
    {
        //
    }
}
```

This is usually from `app/Exceptions/Handler.php`.

As we build up our framework, I want to build something similar, so that the validation exception handling code we added to the router has a more appropriate place to live.

Summary

We tackled a lot in this chapter. We started by adding better error handling and environmental secrets. We followed that up by arranging our application into controllers, so that we don't have to wade through an immense routes file.

Then, we added validation rules and helper functions to run them. Helper functions to redirect this way and that. Helper functions to add CSRF protection to our forms.

What a busy chapter!

In the next chapter, we're going to start working in the database. We'll learn how to connect to various engines, as well as how to read and write to them.

CHAPTER 6

Building a Database Library

In the previous chapter, we built a registration form. Having validated the data, we stopped short of putting that data into the database. We're going to do that in this chapter!

We're going to build a solid foundation for the chapters to come, creating the code that will connect to multiple database engines and execute queries in a safe way. We'll even throw in a migration system. Don't worry if some of this is unfamiliar – we'll go through things at a steady pace.

You're going to need to have access to a MySQL database for most of the code in this chapter to work. Refer back to Chapter 1 for environmental setup details.

What Are Database Libraries Used For?

Perhaps you're assuming that database libraries are only useful for "reading and writing to the database," but they can have a depth to them. For starters, popular database libraries allow developers to use few different database engines with simple configuration changes.

Managing a MySQL database is a bit different from managing a SQLite database and managing a MS SQL Server database. The code written to perform database queries should be able to work with multiple database engines, and folks using a general-purpose database library shouldn't need to write different "queries" based on which database engine they're using.

133

© Christopher Pitt 2021
C. Pitt, *Pro PHP 8 MVC*, https://doi.org/10.1007/978-1-4842-6957-2_6

Additionally, queries should be "secure," which means a good database library will need to escape the data being used in them so that it's difficult to do something insecure. Where possible, prepared statements should be used, for the performance and security benefits they provide.

We're going to build a database library that has all of these benefits.

We'll also take some time to build a migration helper, so that the structure of the database can be committed to code. Migrations aren't strictly a requirement of building a good database library, but they're useful and in the same wheelhouse.

Things We Should Add

Let's enumerate the important features we want to build, so you know what's coming up. Here are the things I think we should add:

- A factory to create the database "driver" specific to the engine we pick in a simple config

- Different "dialects" for speaking to each of the database engines we care about

- Patterns for performing safe database queries (like fetching, inserting, updating, and deleting rows)

- Basic migrations, which will persist new tables or table modifications to each of the database engines we support

---

We don't have to use the Factory pattern to make connections to the database engines, but it's a lot easier to maintain a library where the creation of connections is centralized inside a single class whose job it is to make those connections.

Writing a database library happens in two parts: writing the queries that are commonly used and connecting that code to the underlying drivers that connect to the engine and perform the queries.

We're going to use the PDO (or PHP Data Objects) extension that was added to PHP v5 for the second half of the equation.

Database work is one of the biggest security vulnerability surface areas in web dev, so I highly recommend reviewing the best practices outlined in `https://phptherightway.com/#databases`.

Communicating with the Database

Let's start off by creating the factory class(es), and we'll use a simple configuration format to create the appropriate database engine driver object. We're going to need

- The factory class that creates new connections

- The connection class(es) that represents a connection to a database engine and can generate and execute queries

The factory class looks like this:

```
namespace Framework\Database;

use Closure;
use Framework\Database\Connection\Connection;
use Framework\Database\Exception\ConnectionException;

class Factory
{
    protected array $connectors;

    public function addConnector(string $alias, Closure $connector): static
    {
        $this->connectors[$alias] = $connector;
        return $this;
    }

    public function connect(array $config): Connection
    {
        if (!isset($config['type'])) {
            throw new ConnectionException('type is not defined');
        }
```

```
    $type = $config['type'];

    if (isset($this->connectors[$type])) {
        return $this->connectors[$type]($config);
    }

    throw new ConnectionException('unrecognised type');
    }
}
```

This is from `framework/Database/Factory.php`.

This is similar to the managers we've made before, but it's so slim that I'm not going to call it a manager. This is just a factory. We give it a configuration that hints at the type of database engine we want to connect to, and it passes the rest of the configuration through to an initializer function we define.

If we wanted to open a new connection to a MySQL database, we might want to use code resembling the following:

```
namespace App\Http\Controllers;

use Framework\Database\Factory;
use Framework\Database\Connection\MysqlConnection;

class ShowHomePageController
{
    public function handle()
    {
        $factory = new Factory();

        $factory->addConnector('mysql', function($config) {
            return new MysqlConnection($config);
        });

        $connection = $factory->connect([
            'type' => 'mysql',
            'host' => '127.0.0.1',
            'port' => '3306',
```

```
        'database' => 'pro-php-mvc',
        'username' => 'root',
        'password' => '',
    ]);

    $product = $connection
        ->query()
        ->select()
        ->from('products')
        ->first();

    return view('home', [
        'number' => 42,
        'featured' => $product,
    ]);
    }
}
```

This is from `app/Http/Controllers/ShowHomePageController.php`.

For this code to work, we would need a couple well-designed classes in place. The first kind of class we'd need is one to abstract the connections to different database engines. Something based on an abstract class perhaps:

```
namespace Framework\Database\Connection;

use Framework\Database\QueryBuilder\QueryBuilder;
use Pdo;

abstract class Connection
{
    /**
     * Get the underlying Pdo instance for this connection
     */
    abstract public function pdo(): Pdo;
```

```
/**
 * Start a new query on this connection
 */
abstract public function query(): QueryBuilder;
}
```

This is from `framework/Database/Connection/Connection.php`.

When you think about it, there's not much difference between an abstract class and an interface paired with multiple traits. In this case, I can imagine wanting to add methods to the abstract connection class that would naturally fit with every specific database engine connection.

The differences we might see, between different engines, should be represented in subclasses of this abstract class:

```
namespace Framework\Database\Connection;

use Framework\Database\QueryBuilder\MysqlQueryBuilder;
use InvalidArgumentException;
use Pdo;

class MysqlConnection extends Connection
{
    private Pdo $pdo;

    public function __construct(array $config)
    {
        [
            'host' => $host,
            'port' => $port,
            'database' => $database,
            'username' => $username,
            'password' => $password,
        ] = $config;
```

```
    if (empty($host) || empty($database) || empty($username)) {
        throw new InvalidArgumentException('Connection incorrectly
        configured');
    }

    $this->pdo = new Pdo("mysql:host={$host};port={$port};dbname={$data
    base}", $username, $password);
}

public function pdo(): Pdo
{
    return $this->pdo;
}

public function query(): MysqlQueryBuilder
{
    return new MysqlQueryBuilder($this);
}
}
```

This is from `framework/Database/Connection/MysqlConnection.php`.

MySQL connections require a few parameters to be successful. We can use the array destructuring syntax to assign each key to a local variable and then check that they're present before attempting to make a new connection.

Each connection should create a new query builder specific to the same engine. The SqliteConnection class, for instance, will create a SqliteQueryBuilder instead:

```
namespace Framework\Database\Connection;

use Framework\Database\QueryBuilder\SqliteQueryBuilder;
use InvalidArgumentException;
use Pdo;

class SqliteConnection extends Connection
{
    private Pdo $pdo;
```

```php
    public function __construct(array $config)
    {
        ['path' => $path] = $config;

        if (empty($path)) {
            throw new InvalidArgumentException('Connection incorrectly
            configured');
        }

        $this->pdo = new Pdo("sqlite:{$path}");
    }

    public function pdo(): Pdo
    {
        return $this->pdo;
    }

    public function query(): SqliteQueryBuilder
    {
        return new SqliteQueryBuilder($this);
    }
}
```

This is from `framework/Database/Connection/SqliteConnection.php`.

The second kind of class we need to make should abstract the work of building a SQL query, preparing it, and executing it. Again, we can use an abstract base, because most of the SQL syntax is universal:

```php
namespace Framework\Database\QueryBuilder;

use Framework\Database\Connection\Connection;
use Framework\Database\Exception\QueryException;
use Pdo;
use PdoStatement;
```

```php
abstract class QueryBuilder
{
    protected string $type;
    protected string $columns;
    protected string $table;
    protected int $limit;
    protected int $offset;

    /**
     * Get the underlying Connection instance for this query
     */
    abstract public function connection(): Connection;

    /**
     * Fetch all rows matching the current query
     */
    public function all(): array
    {
        $statement = $this->prepare();
        $statement->execute();

        return $statement->fetchAll(Pdo::FETCH_ASSOC);
    }

    /**
     * Prepare a query against a particular connection
     */
    public function prepare(): PdoStatement
    {
        $query = '';

        if ($this->type === 'select') {
            $query = $this->compileSelect($query);
            $query = $this->compileLimit($query);
        }
```

```php
    if (empty($query)) {
        throw new QueryException('Unrecognised query type');
    }

    return $this->connection->pdo()->prepare($query);
}

/**
 * Add select clause to the query
 */
protected function compileSelect(string $query): string
{
    $query .= " SELECT {$this->columns} FROM {$this->table}";

    return $query;
}

/**
 * Add limit and offset clauses to the query
 */
protected function compileLimit(string $query): string
{
    if ($this->limit) {
        $query .= " LIMIT {$this->limit}";
    }

    if ($this->offset) {
        $query .= " OFFSET {$this->offset}";
    }

    return $query;
}

/**
 * Fetch the first row matching the current query
 */
public function first(): array
{
    $statement = $this->take(1)->prepare();
```

```php
        $statement->execute();

        return $statement->fetchAll(Pdo::FETCH_ASSOC);
    }

    /**
     * Limit a set of query results so that it's possible
     * to fetch a single or limited batch of rows
     */
    public function take(int $limit, int $offset = 0): static
    {
        $this->limit = $limit;
        $this->offset = $offset;

        return $this;
    }

    /**
     * Indicate which table the query is targeting
     */
    public function from(string $table): static
    {
        $this->table = $table;
        return $this;
    }

    /**
     * Indicate the query type is a "select" and remember
     * which fields should be returned by the query
     */
    public function select(string $columns = '*'): static
    {
        $this->type = 'select';
        $this->columns = $columns;

        return $this;
    }
}
```

This is from `framework/Database/QueryBuilder/QueryBuilder.php`.

For this first version of the query builder, we're only supporting select queries. We'll build this up as we go along...

The SQL syntax to select and limit results from a database table is the same in MySQL and SQLite. That means we can have relatively light MySQL and SQLite subclasses:

```php
namespace Framework\Database\QueryBuilder;

use Framework\Database\Connection\MysqlConnection;

class MysqlQueryBuilder extends QueryBuilder
{
    protected MysqlConnection $connection;

    public function __construct(MysqlConnection $connection)
    {
        $this->connection = $connection;
    }
}
```

This is from `framework/Database/QueryBuilder/MysqlQueryBuilder.php`.

```php
namespace Framework\Database\QueryBuilder;

use Framework\Database\Connection\SqliteConnection;

class SqliteQueryBuilder extends QueryBuilder
{
    protected SqliteConnection $connection;

    public function __construct(SqliteConnection $connection)
    {
        $this->connection = $connection;
    }
}
```

This is from `framework/Database/QueryBuilder/SqliteQueryBuilder.php`.

These subclasses do little more than ensure type safety from the factory, but in time they can store more and more engine-specific query syntax.

Now, if we create a temporary "products" table and add a record to it, we should see that record returned and stored in the $product variable.

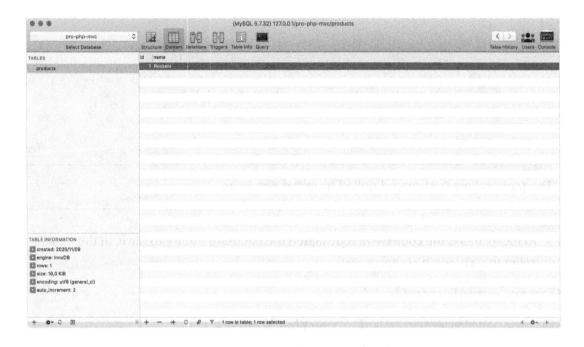

A temporary products table with a single row

```
● ● ●              < > ①              127.0.0.1:8000              ◀) ↻

    Welcome to Whoosh!
    Here, you can buy 42 rockets.

    Array
    (
        [0] => Array
            (
                [id] => 1
                [name] => Rockets
            )

    )
```

The featured product record pulled from the database

To recap, this is the code we first designed the database library to have, in the controller that shows the home page:

```php
$factory = new Factory();

$factory->addConnector('mysql', function($config) {
    return new MysqlConnection($config);
});

$connection = $factory->connect([
    'type' => 'mysql',
    'host' => '127.0.0.1',
    'port' => '3306',
    'database' => 'pro-php-mvc',
    'username' => 'root',
    'password' => '',
]);
```

```
$product = $connection
    ->query()
    ->select()
    ->from('products')
    ->first();
```

This is from app/Http/Controllers/ShowHomePageController.php.

If you're struggling to create the temporary table, use this SQL statement in your database editor of choice:

```
CREATE TABLE `products` (
  `id` int(11) unsigned NOT NULL AUTO_INCREMENT,
  `name` varchar(255) DEFAULT NULL,
  PRIMARY KEY (`id`)
) ENGINE=InnoDB AUTO_INCREMENT=1 DEFAULT CHARSET=utf8;
```

This syntax is unwieldy, though. It would be far better if we had a system for creating and modifying database tables. Let's create a system we can use to do just that!

Running Commands from the Terminal

So far, we've executed other people's commands. Let's set up a few of our own, so that we have a way to extend our applications with administrative functions that can be run from the terminal and potentially on a schedule.

We learned, in the first chapter, that it's possible to run PHP scripts in a number of ways. One of those ways is directly in the terminal. The basics of this are

1. Accepting input from the command that was executed

2. Performing one or more tasks

3. Sending output back to the terminal

Let's try each of these out, by pulling in a name and printing out the name converted to uppercase:

```
$name = $argv[1] ?? 'stranger';
print strtoupper($name) . PHP_EOL;
```

1. Running this with php command.php will print "STRANGER"

2. Running this with php command.php Jeff will print "JEFF"

When designing increasingly complex terminal commands, we're often going to have to deal with inputs. We might want to validate the inputs or allow defaults for optional inputs. We might event want to format the output to make use of the system colors and font variants.

All of these things require more and more custom code or the use of a great library. Let's install Symfony's console library, to abstract these details for us:

```
composer require symfony/console
```

Symfony console applications are built using two main parts. The first is an entry script – similar to public/index.php. The second is one or more "command" classes.

The entry script looks like this:

```
require __DIR__ . '/vendor/autoload.php';

use Dotenv\Dotenv;
use Symfony\Component\Console\Application;

$dotenv = Dotenv::createImmutable(__DIR__);
$dotenv->load();

$application = new Application();

$commands = require __DIR__ . '/app/commands.php';

foreach ($commands as $command) {
    $application->add(new $command);
}

$application->run();
```

This is from `command.php`.

This is a slightly modified form of the example presented in the official Symfony console documentation. The differences are the following:

1. We've enabled the DotEnv secrets we're using in the main application.

2. We're loading in a list of commands from another file.

The list of commands is coming from a file that we can define inside our app directory:

```php
use App\Console\Commands\NameCommand;

return [
    NameCommand::class,
];
```

This is from `app/commands.php`.

The idea behind a file like this is that it provides a way for new commands to be added to the terminal script without modifying that same script. It's entirely reasonable for you to distribute your terminal script alongside your framework, and it might be scary inside there.

You don't necessarily want people digging around in there and potentially breaking how the terminal script works. This file provides a relatively unbreakable experience for folks who want to add their own commands alongside those provided by the framework.

Symfony command classes look like this:

```php
namespace App\Console\Commands;

use Symfony\Component\Console\Command\Command;
use Symfony\Component\Console\Input\InputArgument;
use Symfony\Component\Console\Input\InputInterface;
use Symfony\Component\Console\Output\OutputInterface;
```

```php
class NameCommand extends Command
{
    protected static $defaultName = 'name';

    protected $requireName = false;

    protected function configure()
    {
        $this
            ->setDescription('Prints the name in uppercase')
            ->setHelp('This command takes an optional name and returns it
            in uppercase. If no name is provided, "stranger" is used.')
            ->addArgument('name', $this->requireName ?
            InputArgument::REQUIRED : InputArgument::OPTIONAL, 'Optional
            name');
    }

    protected function execute(InputInterface $input, OutputInterface
    $output)
    {
        $output->writeln(strtoupper($input->getArgument('name') ?:
        'Stranger'));

        return Command::SUCCESS;
    }
}
```

This is from app/Console/Commands/NameCommand.php.

There are three parts to each command:

1. The $defaultName property, which determines the name of the command in the terminal

2. The configure method, which is used to define how the command is called, how it describes itself, and what arguments can be used with it

3. The execute method, where the work of the command happens

I've added the $requireName property and an example of how your commands can define arguments that are optional or required.

It's possible to create the structures that Symfony's console library provides, but that could easily take multiple chapters, for very little gain.

As we'll see later in the book, building larger frameworks and applications is often not about writing all of the code from scratch, especially when it's not an essential part of the goal you're trying to achieve.

Making a Migration Command

Now that we can run our own commands, we can make a command that persists database code structures to a database engine of our choosing. We're going to extend our database library to allow the creation of database tables.

Let's add methods for creating, altering, and deleting tables. It would probably be neater to split the ordinary QueryBuilder code from this migration code, so let's create a new set of classes for handling migrations:

```
namespace Framework\Database\Connection;

use Framework\Database\Migration\Migration;
use Framework\Database\QueryBuilder\QueryBuilder;
use Pdo;

abstract class Connection
{
    /**
     * Get the underlying Pdo instance for this connection
     */
    abstract public function pdo(): Pdo;

    /**
     * Start a new query on this connection
     */
    abstract public function query(): QueryBuilder;
```

```
/**
 * Start a new migration to add a table on this connection
 */
abstract public function createTable(string $table): Migration;
}
```

This new method should kick off a new "create table" migration. It's abstract, so each connection should implement its own version:

```
namespace Framework\Database\Connection;

use Framework\Database\Migration\MysqlMigration;
use Framework\Database\QueryBuilder\MysqlQueryBuilder;
use InvalidArgumentException;
use Pdo;

class MysqlConnection extends Connection
{
    //...

    public function createTable(string $table): MysqlMigration
    {
        return new MysqlMigration($this, $table, 'create');
    }
}
```

This is from `framework/Database/Connection/MysqlConnection.php`.

Migrations, similar to query builders, are going to be based on a common abstract class. Database migrations are all about the different field types that one wants to add to the new table or change in an existing table:

```php
namespace Framework\Database\Migration;

use Framework\Database\Connection\Connection;
use Framework\Database\Migration\Field\BoolField;
use Framework\Database\Migration\Field\DateTimeField;
use Framework\Database\Migration\Field\FloatField;
use Framework\Database\Migration\Field\IdField;
use Framework\Database\Migration\Field\IntField;
use Framework\Database\Migration\Field\StringField;
use Framework\Database\Migration\Field\TextField;

abstract class Migration
{
    protected array $fields = [];

    public function bool(string $name): BoolField
    {
        $field = $this->fields[] = new BoolField($name);
        return $field;
    }

    public function dateTime(string $name): DateTimeField
    {
        $field = $this->fields[] = new DateTimeField($name);
        return $field;
    }

    public function float(string $name): FloatField
    {
        $field = $this->fields[] = new FloatField($name);
        return $field;
    }

    public function id(string $name): IdField
    {
        $field = $this->fields[] = new IdField($name);
        return $field;
    }
```

```php
    public function int(string $name): IntField
    {
        $field = $this->fields[] = new IntField($name);
        return $field;
    }

    public function string(string $name): StringField
    {
        $field = $this->fields[] = new StringField($name);
        return $field;
    }

    public function text(string $name): TextField
    {
        $field = $this->fields[] = new TextField($name);
        return $field;
    }

    abstract public function connection(): Connection;
    abstract public function execute(): void;
}
```

This is from `framework/Database/Migration/Migration.php`.

All of these methods do pretty much the same thing. The reason for all the duplication is to provide type hinting for each field type, so that development tools can correctly analyze and alert when they are used incorrectly.

I'm not going to go through all of the database engine implementations for migrations, because it's loads of code that aren't particularly interesting. If you're curious, check out the `SqliteMigration` class and the `Field` subclasses I don't mention...

Each of these fields is based on an abstract `Field` class:

```php
namespace Framework\Database\Migration\Field;

abstract class Field
{
    public string $name;
    public bool $nullable = false;

    public function __construct(string $name)
    {
        $this->name = $name;
    }

    public function nullable(): static
    {
        $this->nullable = true;
        return $this;
    }
}
```

This is from `framework/Database/Migration/Field/Field.php`.

I'm a bit torn by this architecture. On the one hand, it's cool that all nullable fields can have their `nullable` method defined here – it saves needless duplication. On the other hand, I can't define a method people can use to specify default column values, because I want those to be type specific:

```php
namespace Framework\Database\Migration\Field;

class BoolField extends Field
{
    public bool $default;

    public function default(bool $value): static
    {
```

```
        $this->default = $value;
        return $this;
    }
}
```

This is from `framework/Database/Migration/Field/BoolField.php`.

Here, we're making the `default` method only accept Boolean values, and we'd struggle to define that as an abstract method on `Field` *or* to define a type-less method on `Field` that can then be correctly typed from the subclass.

We can define the `nullable` method on `Field`, because it requires no types as arguments.

Both of these methods (`nullable` and `default`) suffer from another problem – fields that don't allow these operations need to have special exception handling:

```
namespace Framework\Database\Migration\Field;

use Framework\Database\Exception\MigrationException;

class IdField extends Field
{
    public function default()
    {
        throw new MigrationException('ID fields cannot have a default
        value');
    }
}
```

This is from `framework/Database/Migration/Field/IdField.php`.

On their own, these fields don't do very much to the database. Even if they did, they'd run into differences in the database engines, which might lead to another level of abstraction (fields for each database engine).

Instead, our migration classes can interpret the different field types:

```php
namespace Framework\Database\Migration;

use Framework\Database\Connection\MysqlConnection;
use Framework\Database\Exception\MigrationException;
use Framework\Database\Migration\Field\Field;
use Framework\Database\Migration\Field\BoolField;
use Framework\Database\Migration\Field\DateTimeField;
use Framework\Database\Migration\Field\FloatField;
use Framework\Database\Migration\Field\IdField;
use Framework\Database\Migration\Field\IntField;
use Framework\Database\Migration\Field\StringField;
use Framework\Database\Migration\Field\TextField;

class MysqlMigration extends Migration
{
    protected MysqlConnection $connection;
    protected string $table;
    protected string $type;

    public function __construct(MysqlConnection $connection, string $table,
    string $type)
    {
        $this->connection = $connection;
        $this->table = $table;
        $this->type = $type;
    }

    public function execute()
    {
        $fields = array_map(fn($field) => $this->stringForField($field),
        $this->fields);
        $fields = join(',' . PHP_EOL, $fields);

        $primary = array_filter($this->fields, fn($field) => $field
        instanceof IdField);
```

```php
    $primaryKey = isset($primary[0]) ? "PRIMARY KEY (`{$primary[0]->
    name}`)" : '';

    $query = "
        CREATE TABLE `{$this->table}` (
            {$fields},
            {$primaryKey}
        ) ENGINE=InnoDB AUTO_INCREMENT=1 DEFAULT CHARSET=utf8;
    ";

    $statement = $this->connection->pdo()->prepare($query);
    $statement->execute();
}

private function stringForField(Field $field): string
{
    if ($field instanceof BoolField) {
        $template = "`{$field->name}` tinyint(4)";

        if ($field->nullable) {
            $template .= " DEFAULT NULL";
        }

        if ($field->default !== null) {
            $default = (int) $field->default;
            $template .= " DEFAULT {$default}";
        }

        return $template;
    }

    if ($field instanceof DateTimeField) {
        $template = "`{$field->name}` datetime";

        if ($field->nullable) {
            $template .= " DEFAULT NULL";
        }
```

```
        if ($field->default === 'CURRENT_TIMESTAMP') {
            $template .= " DEFAULT CURRENT_TIMESTAMP";
        } else if ($field->default !== null) {
            $template .= " DEFAULT '{$field->default}'";
        }

        return $template;
    }

    if ($field instanceof FloatField) {
        $template = "`{$field->name}` float";

        if ($field->nullable) {
            $template .= " DEFAULT NULL";
        }

        if ($field->default !== null) {
            $template .= " DEFAULT '{$field->default}'";
        }

        return $template;
    }

    if ($field instanceof IdField) {
        return "`{$field->name}` int(11) unsigned NOT NULL AUTO_
        INCREMENT";
    }

    if ($field instanceof IntField) {
        $template = "`{$field->name}` int(11)";

        if ($field->nullable) {
            $template .= " DEFAULT NULL";
        }

        if ($field->default !== null) {
            $template .= " DEFAULT '{$field->default}'";
        }

        return $template;
    }
```

```php
        if ($field instanceof StringField) {
            $template = "`{$field->name}` varchar(255)";

            if ($field->nullable) {
                $template .= " DEFAULT NULL";
            }

            if ($field->default !== null) {
                $template .= " DEFAULT '{$field->default}'";
            }

            return $template;
        }

        if ($field instanceof TextField) {
            return "`{$field->name}` text";
        }

        throw new MigrationException("Unrecognised field type for
        {$field->name}");
    }
}
```

This is from `framework/Database/Migration/MysqlMigration.php`.

The majority of this code lives in the `stringForField` method, so let's start with that. It takes in a `Field` (which could be any of the `Field` subclasses, like `StringField` and `BoolField`) and generates MySQL-compatible syntax to create the field.

It's not an exhaustive reference. There are probably many edge cases that this code doesn't cater for, but it should be good enough for the 80% use case.

It would be nicer for the field classes to define their own syntax – to avoid all this `instanceof` switching – but the syntax differs between engines. We'd need fields that understand all the engines at once or a StringField for each engine...

The execute method calls stringForField for each field, generating a full list of fields that need to be added. It wraps those with the MySQL version of the CREATE TABLE statement. Again, there are many things we could do to extend this:

- Handling custom character sets

- Handling different MySQL table types

- Handling custom auto-number offsets

Feel free to extend it to handle as many of these as you'd like. You have a great place to start from!

You can use this migration code like this:

```
$orders = $connection->createTable('orders');
$orders->id('id');
$orders->int('quantity')->default(1);
$orders->float('price')->nullable();
$orders->bool('is_confirmed')->default(false);
$orders->dateTime('ordered_at')->default('CURRENT_TIMESTAMP');
$orders->text('notes');
$orders->execute();
```

Let's put this inside a "migration" file, so that we can run this (and other migrations) from the command line:

```
use Framework\Database\Connection\Connection;

class CreateOrdersTable
{
    public function migrate(Connection $connection)
    {
        $table = $connection->createTable('orders');
        $table->id('id');
        $table->int('quantity')->default(1);
        $table->float('price')->nullable();
        $table->bool('is_confirmed')->default(false);
        $table->dateTime('ordered_at')->default('CURRENT_TIMESTAMP');
```

```
        $table->text('notes');
        $table->execute();
    }
}
```

This is from database/migrations/001_CreateOrdersTable.php.

I can imagine creating multiple files like this, each describing a change to the database. This way, we can trace the shape of the database over time and get an idea of what it should look like when all the migrations are run in order.

We should create a new command and add it to the list of commands our application knows about. This command needs to

1. Find all migration files.

2. Open a connection to the database.

3. "Migrate" each migration file, giving it the active connection.

Perhaps something like this:

```
namespace Framework\Database\Command;

use Framework\Database\Factory;
use Framework\Database\Connection\MysqlConnection;
use Framework\Database\Connection\SqliteConnection;
use Symfony\Component\Console\Command\Command;
use Symfony\Component\Console\Input\InputArgument;
use Symfony\Component\Console\Input\InputInterface;
use Symfony\Component\Console\Output\OutputInterface;

class MigrateCommand extends Command
{
    protected static $defaultName = 'migrate';

    protected function configure()
    {
        $this
            ->setDescription('Migrates the database')
```

```
        ->setHelp('This command looks for all migration files and runs
        them');
}

protected function execute(InputInterface $input, OutputInterface
$output)
{
    $current = getcwd();
    $pattern = 'database/migrations/*.php';

    $paths = glob("{$current}/{$pattern}");

    if (count($paths) === 0) {
        $this->writeln('No migrations found');
        return Command::SUCCESS;
    }

    $factory = new Factory();

    $factory->addConnector('mysql', function($config) {
        return new MysqlConnection($config);
    });

    $connection = $factory->connect([
        'type' => 'mysql',
        'host' => '127.0.0.1',
        'port' => '3306',
        'database' => 'pro-php-mvc',
        'username' => 'root',
        'password' => '',
    ]);

    foreach ($paths as $path) {
        [$prefix, $file] = explode('_', $path);
        [$class, $extension] = explode('.', $file);

        require $path;
```

```
        $obj = new $class();
        $obj->migrate($connection);
    }

    return Command::SUCCESS;
    }
}
```

This is from `framework/Database/Command/MigrateCommand.php`.

This command operates under the assumption that the `command.php` script will be run when the user is in the same folder: by using the `getcwd()` function. This function returns the current folder path that PHP is being run in.

On top of this, we're looking for all migration files in the `database/migrations` folder, relative to the current path. If none are found, then we don't even bother with the database connection.

If there are migrations to run, we can open a connection and pass it to each migration class's `migrate()` method.

A problem with this approach is that it hard-codes the choice to use MySQL. We really need a way to define a "default" connection, so that we don't need to hard-code the choice.

We're going to build a robust configuration solution in Chapter 11, but for now, we can use something a bit simpler:

```
return [
    'default' => 'mysql',
    'mysql' => [
        'type' => 'mysql',
        'host' => '127.0.0.1',
        'port' => '3306',
        'database' => 'pro-php-mvc',
        'username' => 'root',
        'password' => '',
    ],
```

```
    'sqlite' => [
        'type' => 'sqlite',
        'path' => __DIR__ . '/../database/database.sqlite',
    ],
];
```

This is from `config/database.php`.

Now, we can require this "config" file wherever we need the database credentials:

```
namespace App\Http\Controllers;

use Framework\Database\Factory;
use Framework\Database\Connection\MysqlConnection;
use Framework\Database\Connection\SqliteConnection;

class ShowHomePageController
{
    public function handle()
    {
        $factory = new Factory();

        $factory->addConnector('mysql', function($config) {
            return new MysqlConnection($config);
        });

        $factory->addConnector('sqlite', function($config) {
            return new SqliteConnection($config);
        });

        $config = require __DIR__ . '/../../../config/database.php';

        $connection = $factory->connect($config[$config['default']]);

        $product = $connection
            ->query()
            ->select()
            ->from('products')
            ->first();
```

```
        return view('home', [
            'number' => 42,
            'featured' => $product,
        ]);
    }
}
```

This is from app/Http/Controllers/ShowHomePageController.php.

It's still not perfect – we still have to add connection callbacks to the factory every time – but at least the config determines the ideal connector to use. We'll come up with a better way of "building up" the factory in Chapter 10.

We can refactor the MigrateCommand class to use a similar configuration approach:

```
protected function execute(InputInterface $input, OutputInterface $output)
{
    $current = getcwd();
    $pattern = 'database/migrations/*.php';

    $paths = glob("{$current}/{$pattern}");

    if (count($paths) < 1) {
        $this->writeln('No migrations found');
        return Command::SUCCESS;
    }

    $connection = $this->connection();

    foreach ($paths as $path) {
        [$prefix, $file] = explode('_', $path);
        [$class, $extension] = explode('.', $file);

        require $path;

        $obj = new $class();
        $obj->migrate($connection);
    }
```

```php
        return Command::SUCCESS;
}

private function connection(): Connection
{
    $factory = new Factory();

    $factory->addConnector('mysql', function($config) {
        return new MysqlConnection($config);
    });

    $factory->addConnector('sqlite', function($config) {
        return new SqliteConnection($config);
    });

    $config = require getcwd() . '/config/database.php';

    return $factory->connect($config[$config['default']]);
}
```

This is from framework/Database/Command/MigrateCommand.php.

Before we can run this command, we need to add it to the list of known commands:

```php
use App\Console\Commands\NameCommand;
use Framework\Database\Command\MigrateCommand;

return [
    MigrateCommand::class,
    NameCommand::class,
];
```

This is from app/commands.php.

Altering Tables

Migrations aren't only for creating tables. They also need to be able to alter tables, by changing and dropping columns when the application requires it.

We can add to the existing migrations to support this, starting with altering fields

```
/**
 * Start a new migration to add a table on this connection
 */
abstract public function alterTable(string $table): Migration;
```

This is from `framework/Database/Connection/Connection.php`.

...and in the different engine subclasses:

```
public function alterTable(string $table): MysqlMigration
{
    return new MysqlMigration($this, $table, 'alter');
}
```

This is from `framework/Database/Connection/MysqlConnection.php`.

We also need to change how the field definitions are defined, to allow them to be added to existing tables and to allow them to be modified:

```
private function stringForField(Field $field): string
{
    $prefix = '';

    if ($this->type === 'alter') {
        $prefix = 'ADD';
    }

    if ($field->alter) {
        $prefix = 'MODIFY';
    }
```

```php
if ($field instanceof BoolField) {
    $template = "{$prefix} `{$field->name}` tinyint(4)";

    if ($field->nullable) {
        $template .= " DEFAULT NULL";
    }

    if ($field->default !== null) {
        $default = (int) $field->default;
        $template .= " DEFAULT {$default}";
    }

    return $template;
}

if ($field instanceof DateTimeField) {
    $template = "{$prefix} `{$field->name}` datetime";

    if ($field->nullable) {
        $template .= " DEFAULT NULL";
    }

    if ($field->default === 'CURRENT_TIMESTAMP') {
        $template .= " DEFAULT CURRENT_TIMESTAMP";
    } else if ($field->default !== null) {
        $template .= " DEFAULT '{$field->default}'";
    }

    return $template;
}

if ($field instanceof FloatField) {
    $template = "{$prefix} `{$field->name}` float";

    if ($field->nullable) {
        $template .= " DEFAULT NULL";
    }

    if ($field->default !== null) {
        $template .= " DEFAULT '{$field->default}'";
    }
```

```
        return $template;
    }

    if ($field instanceof IdField) {
        return "{$prefix} `{$field->name}` int(11) unsigned NOT NULL AUTO_
        INCREMENT";
    }

    if ($field instanceof IntField) {
        $template = "{$prefix} `{$field->name}` int(11)";

        if ($field->nullable) {
            $template .= " DEFAULT NULL";
        }

        if ($field->default !== null) {
            $template .= " DEFAULT '{$field->default}'";
        }

        return $template;
    }

    if ($field instanceof StringField) {
        $template = "{$prefix} `{$field->name}` varchar(255)";

        if ($field->nullable) {
            $template .= " DEFAULT NULL";
        }

        if ($field->default !== null) {
            $template .= " DEFAULT '{$field->default}'";
        }

        return $template;
    }

    if ($field instanceof TextField) {
        return "{$prefix} `{$field->name}` text";
    }

    throw new MigrationException("Unrecognised field type for {$field->name}");
}
```

This is from `framework/Database/Migration/MysqlMigration.php`.

The only significant change is that we're determining the prefix for each field definition (either `ADD` or `MODIFY`), when the migration is an alteration.

Similarly, we need to refactor the `execute` method, to generate very different queries depending on whether the migration is creating or altering the table:

```php
public function execute()
{
    $fields = array_map(fn($field) => $this->stringForField($field),
    $this->fields);

    $primary = array_filter($this->fields, fn($field) => $field instanceof
    IdField);
    $primaryKey = isset($primary[0]) ? "PRIMARY KEY (`{$primary[0]->
    name}`)" : '';

    if ($this->type === 'create') {
        $fields = join(PHP_EOL, array_map(fn($field) => "{$field},",
        $fields));

        $query = "
            CREATE TABLE `{$this->table}` (
                {$fields}
                {$primaryKey}
            ) ENGINE=InnoDB AUTO_INCREMENT=1 DEFAULT CHARSET=utf8;
        ";
    }

    if ($this->type === 'alter') {
        $fields = join(PHP_EOL, array_map(fn($field) => "{$field};",
        $fields));

        $query = "
            ALTER TABLE `{$this->table}`
            {$fields}
        ";
    }
```

```
    $statement = $this->connection->pdo()->prepare($query);
    $statement->execute();
}
```

This is from `framework/Database/Migration/MysqlMigration.php`.

The fields also need different separators between them: `,` for create queries and `;` for alter queries. The SQLite migration class has similar changes, but it also limits altering columns (because SQLite doesn't allow that kind of change).

Finally, we can allow for dropping columns, by adding a new `Migration` method:

```
abstract public function dropColumn(string $name): static;
```

This is from `framework/Database/Migration/Migration.php`.

The reason we want this to be abstract is that different engines have their own restrictions for dropping columns. SQLite, for instance, doesn't allow for dropping columns, so we can throw an exception in that case.

Technically, it is possible to drop a column, by recreating the table and transferring over the row data that remains, but it's a pain in the butt…

```
protected MysqlConnection $connection;
protected string $table;
protected string $type;
protected array $drops = [];

//...

public function dropColumn(string $name): static
{
    $this->drops[] = $name;
    return $this;
}
```

This is from `framework/Database/Migration/MysqlMigration.php`.

And then we need to allow these "drops" to be added to the alteration queries:

```php
public function execute()
{
    $fields = array_map(fn($field) => $this->stringForField($field),
    $this->fields);

    $primary = array_filter($this->fields, fn($field) => $field instanceof
    IdField);
    $primaryKey = isset($primary[0]) ? "PRIMARY KEY (`{$primary[0]-
    >name}`)" : '';

    if ($this->type === 'create') {
        $fields = join(PHP_EOL, array_map(fn($field) => "{$field},",
        $fields));

        $query = "
            CREATE TABLE `{$this->table}` (
                {$fields}
                {$primaryKey}
            ) ENGINE=InnoDB AUTO_INCREMENT=1 DEFAULT CHARSET=utf8;
        ";
    }

    if ($this->type === 'alter') {
        $fields = join(PHP_EOL, array_map(fn($field) => "{$field};",
        $fields));
        $drops = join(PHP_EOL, array_map(fn($drop) => "DROP COLUMN
        `{$drop}`;", $this->drops));

        $query = "
            ALTER TABLE `{$this->table}`
            {$fields}
            {$drops}
        ";
    }
```

```
$statement = $this->connection->pdo()->prepare($query);
$statement->execute();
}
```

This is from `framework/Database/Migration/MysqlMigration.php`.

Let's call it there. We've achieved a lot in this chapter, and it's time to reflect and experiment.

Caveats

This is a great place to start from, but it's not bulletproof. There are a number of ways we can improve what we've built in this chapter and avoid common error conditions:

1. By supporting more database engines

2. By extending the query syntax to allow for groups and more types of conditions and "raw" query fragments

3. By creating a "migrations" database table, to track which migrations have already been run, so that we don't try to recreate existing tables

4. By adding "path" helpers, so we don't depend on `getcwd()` for finding config and migrations

5. By formalizing the interface through which new connectors are defined

6. By type-checking more of the configuration parameters, so that we're certain about data types and shapes before trying to use them to connect

7. By validating migration file names or making the class name inference more robust

I'd consider all of these interesting next steps after what we've already achieved. Go on and try one or two of them...

How the Pros Do It

Much of what I've shown you is inspired by frameworks like Laravel. Laravel has an extensive database library, migration system, and other goodies that make working with the database a lovely experience.

It has a few different command-line tools, for things like seeding the database with dummy data and running all migrations from scratch (so you don't have to manually "clear out the database" before running the migrations again).

Furthermore, Laravel's migrations look like this:

```php
use Illuminate\Database\Migrations\Migration;
use Illuminate\Database\Schema\Blueprint;
use Illuminate\Support\Facades\Schema;

class CreateUsersTable extends Migration
{
    public function up()
    {
        Schema::create('users', function (Blueprint $table) {
            $table->id();
            $table->string('name');
            $table->string('email')->unique();
            $table->timestamp('email_verified_at')->nullable();
            $table->string('password');
            $table->rememberToken();
            $table->timestamps();
        });
    }

    public function down()
    {
        Schema::dropIfExists('users');
    }
}
```

...where the up() method is run when the migrations are "normally" run and the down() method is run when they are reversed or a "fresh" run is requested.

Other database libraries have different (non-PHP methods of defining migrations). Defining a "table" in Propel looks like this:

```
<database name="bookstore" defaultIdMethod="native">
  <table name="book" description="Book Table">
    <column name="id" type="integer" primaryKey="true" autoIncrement="true" />
    <column name="title" type="varchar" required="true"
    primaryString="true" />
    <column name="isbn" required="true" type="varchar" size="24"
    phpName="ISBN" />
  </table>
</database>
```

It's not my favorite approach to defining table structures, but it works. Still, other database libraries (like the one inside SilverStripe) don't have any visible migrations. There, you define the table structure "inline":

```
use SilverStripe\ORM\DataObject;

class Player extends DataObject
{
    private static $db = [
        'PlayerNumber' => 'Int',
        'FirstName' => 'Varchar(255)',
        'LastName' => 'Text',
        'Birthday' => 'Date'
    ];
}
```

The migrations that are performed follow a set of conventions, and they can perform destructive operations like removing tables or columns. You need to study their documentation carefully before making changes to inline table definitions...

These kinds of frameworks usually have a small set of all-encompassing "cache" commands that build and persist everything required for the application to function.

Summary

In this chapter, we did a lot of heavy lifting. We built a database library, using PDO under the hood, that abstracts the connection and query process.

We added command-line support, so our framework can begin to define useful processes to kick off in the terminal. We also built a way to define database structures in code and connected those structures to the command line.

In the next chapter, we're going to take all this one step further and build representations of the database rows in PHP objects. We're going to build our own ORM.

CHAPTER 7

Building an Object-Relational Mapper Library

In the previous chapter, we built a solid foundation for database work. We have a driver-based database library, through which we can execute SQL queries in an engine-agnostic way.

In this chapter, we're going to take things even further. We're going to build an Object-Relational Mapper (or ORM) library, to represent database rows and tables as PHP objects.

We've built enough of our framework, and Whoosh! website, that there are a bunch improvements we could be making to the website design and functionality. Instead of taking up time doing that in this book, I'm going to start doing much of that work between chapters.

In the Meantime…

Before we get deep into the ORM library, I want to talk about what has changed since the previous chapter's code.

You can find the code for the changes I'm about to discuss on GitHub. I'm going to follow this pattern of between-chapter-x-and-y for code that happens between chapters.

179

© Christopher Pitt 2021
C. Pitt, *Pro PHP 8 MVC*, https://doi.org/10.1007/978-1-4842-6957-2_7

Redesigned Registration, Home, and Product Pages

I thought it was time to improve on the visual design of these pages. I'm no designer, but I think Tailwind provides a bunch of tools to make visual design easier.

I took a trip to undraw.co to find an illustration of a rocket and created a couple different "feature" includes. I also listed the products on the home page and added a button for ordering each...

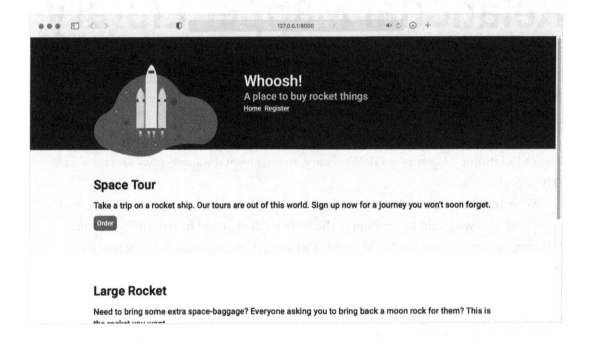

The new home page design

The registration page got a facelift, using the smaller "feature" include, and now includes a login form.

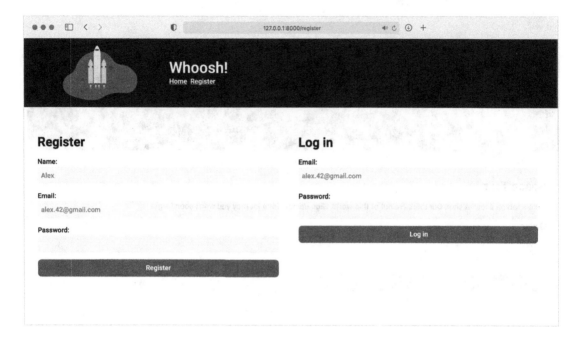

The new register page

Finally, I changed the product page to include an order form. It's going to need some login to only show the order form to authenticated users, but it's in a fine place for us to work in it.

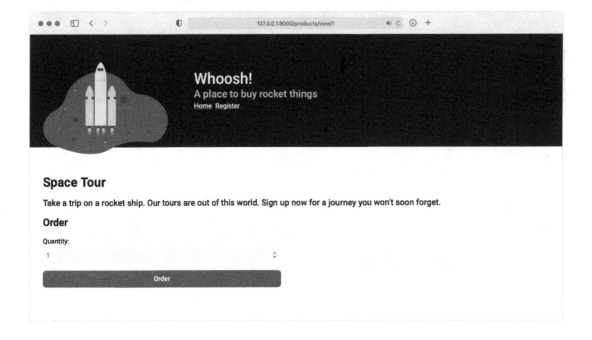

The new order page

New Migrate Flag and Seeding

I thought it was time for us to build the products table in a migration and populate it
with example products. This process of populating migration tables with example data is
called seeding. It's not a very different process in code:

```
use Framework\Database\Connection\Connection;

class SeedProducts
{
    public function migrate(Connection $connection)
    {
        $products = [
            [
                'name' => 'Space Tour',
```

```
            'description' => 'Take a trip on a rocket ship. Our tours
            are out of this world. Sign up now for a journey you
            won&apos;t soon forget.',
        ],
        [
            'name' => 'Large Rocket',
            'description' => 'Need to bring some extra space-baggage?
            Everyone asking you to bring back a moon rock for them?
            This is the rocket you want...',
        ],
        [
            'name' => 'Small Rocket',
            'description' => 'Space exploration is expensive. This
            rocket comes in under budget and atmosphere.',
        ],
    ];

    foreach ($products as $product) {
        $connection
            ->query()
            ->from('products')
            ->insert(['name', 'description'], $product);
    }
  }
}
```

This is from database/migrations/006_SeedProducts.php.

This code depends on a couple important changes to the database structure and library. The migration to add the products table looks like this:

```
use Framework\Database\Connection\Connection;

class CreateProductsTable
{
    public function migrate(Connection $connection)
```

```
    {
        $table = $connection->createTable('products');
        $table->id('id');
        $table->string('name');
        $table->text('description');
        $table->execute();
    }
}
```

This is from database/migrations/005_CreateProductsTable.php.

The next big change was the introduction of a method to insert new database records:

```
protected array $values;

public function insert(array $columns, array $values): int
{
    $this->type = 'insert';
    $this->columns = $columns;
    $this->values = $values;

    $statement = $this->prepare();

    return $statement->execute($values);
}

public function prepare(): PdoStatement
{
    // ...

    if ($this->type === 'insert') {
        $query = $this->compileInsert($query);
    }

    // ...
}
```

```php
protected function compileInsert(string $query): string
{
    $joinedColumns = join(', ', $this->columns);
    $joinedPlaceholders = join(', ', array_map(fn($column) => ":{$column}",
    $this->columns));

    $query .= " INSERT INTO {$this->table} ({$joinedColumns}) VALUES
    ({$joinedPlaceholders})";

    return $query;
}
```

This is from framework/Database/QueryBuilder/QueryBuilder.php.

This code is pretty similar to the SQL "select" code we did before, but it uses a feature of PDO prepared statements where values are inserted through the use of placeholders. The following SQL statement tells PDO to expect values in the placeholders:

INSERT INTO products (name, description) **VALUES** (:name, :description)

These values are sent through with the following code:

```php
$sql = "...the above SQL statement";

$values = [
    'name' => $name,
    'description' => $description,
];

$affectedRows = $pdo->prepare($sql)->execute($values);
```

I also changed the `protected array $columns` property to expect an array instead of a string and made the corresponding change to the `select` method.

It got a bit annoying manually deleting tables to verify these changes, so I added a new flag to the `migrate` command, so we can now go

```php
php command.php migrate --fresh
```

The migrate command also now creates a `migrations` table, so that migrations are only run if they haven't already been run (or if the `--fresh` flag is present):

```
protected function configure()
{
    $this
        ->setDescription('Migrates the database')
        ->addOption('fresh', null, InputOption::VALUE_NONE, 'Delete all
        tables before running the migrations')
        ->setHelp('This command looks for all migration files and runs
        them');
}

protected function execute(InputInterface $input, OutputInterface $output)
{
    // ...get the migration files and connection

    if ($input->getOption('fresh')) {
        $output->writeln('Dropping existing database tables');

        $connection->dropTables();
        $connection = $this->connection();
    }

    if (!$connection->hasTable('migrations')) {
        $output->writeln('Creating migrations table');
        $this->createMigrationsTable($connection);
    }

    foreach ($paths as $path) {
        // ...run the migration

        $connection
            ->query()
            ->from('migrations')
            ->insert(['name'], ['name' => $class]);
    }

    return Command::SUCCESS;
}
```

```php
private function createMigrationsTable(Connection $connection)
{
    $table = $connection->createTable('migrations');
    $table->id('id');
    $table->string('name');
    $table->execute();
}
```

This is from framework/Database/Command/MigrateCommand.php.

This meant I also had to add methods to the Connection classes, to find tables and drop them:

```php
/**
 * Return a  list of table names on this connection
 */
abstract public function getTables(): array;

/**
 * Find out if a table exists on this connection
 */
abstract public function hasTable(string $name): bool;

/**
 * Drop all tables in the current database
 */
abstract public function dropTables(): int;
```

This is from framework/Database/Connection/Connection.php.

The approaches vary by database engine, so check out how MysqlConnection and SqliteConnection achieve these methods, if it interests you.

The `SqliteConnection->dropTables` method has a caveat: it will only drop tables if the file path is not `:memory:`. You see, it's possible to have an in-memory SQLite database, which isn't stored in the filesystem and which needs a more complex `dropTables` implementation.

Validation Errors and the Session

I also made a small change to the validation error handling. It's now possible to choose a name by which errors will be stored in the session. This makes it possible to have multiple forms on the same page and display form errors separately.

Controllers

Along with a better design of the forms, I had to change some of the controller code. This was mostly a process of moving the `csrf` call to the controllers (so that they can be used in multiple forms on the same page) and sending the form actions (routes) from the controller.

I also added a way to send "where" clauses to the `QueryBuilder` class and changed how single rows are returned:

```
protected array $wheres = [];

public function all(): array
{
    $statement = $this->prepare();
    $statement->execute($this->getWhereValues());

    return $statement->fetchAll(Pdo::FETCH_ASSOC);
}

protected function getWhereValues(): array
{
    $values = [];

    if (count($this->wheres) === 0) {
        return $values;
    }
```

```php
    foreach ($this->wheres as $where) {
        $values[$where[0]] = $where[2];
    }

    return $values;
}

public function prepare(): PdoStatement
{
    $query = '';

    if ($this->type === 'select') {
        $query = $this->compileSelect($query);
        $query = $this->compileWheres($query);
        $query = $this->compileLimit($query);
    }

    // ...
}

protected function compileWheres(string $query): string
{
    if (count($this->wheres) === 0) {
        return $query;
    }

    $query .= ' WHERE';

    foreach ($this->wheres as $i => $where) {
        if ($i > 0) {
            $query .= ', ';
        }

        [$column, $comparator, $value] = $where;

        $query .= " {$column} {$comparator} :{$column}";
    }

    return $query;
}
```

```php
public function first(): array
{
    $statement = $this->take(1)->prepare();
    $statement->execute($this->getWhereValues());

    $result = $statement->fetchAll(Pdo::FETCH_ASSOC);

    if (count($result) === 1) {
        return $result[0];
    }

    return null;
}
```

This is from `framework/Database/QueryBuilder/QueryBuilder.php`.

This uses the same ":placeholder" syntax, to define where clauses. We could provide a lot of similar functionality, for easier handling of nulls and "likes" and so on.

These are the big changes since last chapters. Take some time to go through the code, and see how I solved the challenges I set for you toward the end of the previous chapter.

Why Not Stop with Just a Database Library?

As you've seen, from the previous chapter and the work I've done since then, the database library is already quite powerful. Sure, we could package it up a bit better – so that there isn't so much boilerplate when we want a new connection – but it's already nice to use and to extend.

So why do we need anything more?

Much of the work we do, as PHP developers, involves storing and retrieving data from a database. This happens in two phases:

1. Extracting data from the database or writing to it

2. Transforming data that needs to be written to the database or has just been read from it

On top of this, we will often need to group associated bits of database data by foreign keys. Relational database engines generally provide a way to select based on these kinds of relationships, but they don't represent related rows in a useful way.

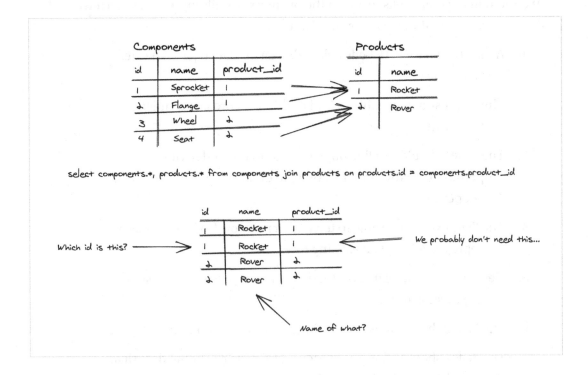

Confusing queries…

While it's true that a more complex query can help to avoid this kind of confusing situation (and the SQL query errors that go along with it), it doesn't need to be this difficult to access both related data types.

We'd be better off with something that takes queries on database rows and gives us back separate data types (or objects) representing each database row.

Those objects can also represent lists of objects (which map to the underlying database rows), but we can take advantage of PHP structures (like iterators and getters/setters) to make working with the underlying rows easier.

Our database library is great for extracting data from and writing data to a database, but its responsibilities don't extend to representing rows (and related rows) as PHP objects.

This is where the term Object-Relational Mapper comes from. At their core, ORMs are about representing the relationships between objects (which represent database rows).

We could fill several books just with the business of building an ORM, so it would be wise to constrain our efforts to a few core features:

1. An abstract base PHP `Model` class that each "data type" can extend and customize.

2. The `Model` should be able to find multiple records, or a single row, via SQL "where" clauses.

3. The `Model` should provide object access to the underlying properties of the row and the ability to define getters or setters for the properties.

4. The `Model` should be able to tell if it's a new row (to be created) or the representation of an existing row.

5. New rows should be inserted; existing row representations should update existing rows.

6. The `Model` should allow for casting row values to non-string types.

7. The `Model` should allow the retrieval of simple relational data (like "has one," "has many," and "belongs to").

"has...one?"

These relationship types aren't specific to PHP or ORMs, but they're important to understand. When linking database rows, we can describe their relationships depending on how the data is defined and what it means.

A "has one" relationship is a way of saying that the row you care about is referenced in another row (probably even a row in another table). An example might help:

1. Princess Peach is the ruler of the Mushroom Kingdom.

2. The Mushroom Kingdom belongs to Princess Peach.

3. Therefore, Princess Peach "has one" kingdom.

We know, from history, that rulers can rule over multiple kingdoms. In a situation where Princess Peach ruled over multiple kingdoms, we'd probably need to represent the relationship as one-to-many. **One** Princess Peach **to many** kingdoms...

It might be represented in the following database structure:

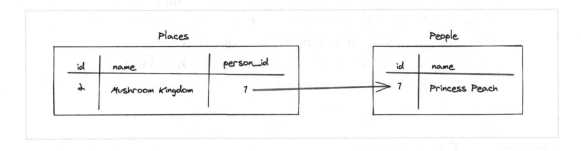

"has one" relationships

A "belongs to" relationship is just the reverse of this. We say that Princess Peach "has one" Mushroom Kingdom, but we can also say the Mushroom Kingdom "belongs to" Princess Peach.

A "has many" relationship is when multiple rows belong to one row.

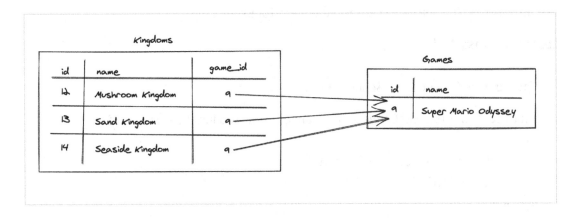

"has many"

This relationship is a bit different:

1. Super Mario Odyssey takes place in a few different kingdoms.

2. Each kingdom "belongs to" the game Super Mario Odyssey.

3. Super Mario Odyssey "has many" kingdoms.

   It's also possible for these kingdoms to feature in multiple games, in which case the relationship would become one of many-to-many. **Many** kingdoms **belonging to many** games. We're not going to venture that deep into relationships in our ORM, because it's much more complex to implement for very little benefit.

Putting It Together

Let's begin with the abstract base Model class. We can make it set up the default connection and subclass it a couple times for orders and products:

```
namespace Framework\Database;

use Framework\Database\Connection\Connection;
use Framework\Database\Connection\MysqlConnection;
use Framework\Database\Connection\SqliteConnection;
use Framework\Database\Exception\ConnectionException;

abstract class Model
{
    protected Connection $connection;

    public function setConnection(Connection $connection): static
    {
        $this->connection = $connection;
        return $this;
    }

    public function getConnection(): Connection
    {
        if (!isset($this->connection)) {
            $factory = new Factory();
```

```
    $factory->addConnector('mysql', function($config) {
        return new MysqlConnection($config);
    });

    $factory->addConnector('sqlite', function($config) {
        return new SqliteConnection($config);
    });

    $config = require basePath() . 'config/database.php';

    $this->connection = $factory->connect($config[$config
    ['default']]);
    }

    return $this->connection;
    }
}
```

This is from `framework/Database/Model.php`.

The first methods we've added allow the overriding of the database connection the model will use, but also provide a default connection to work with. This will save us a fair bit of boilerplate.

It's still not the final solution, when it comes to setting up new database connections, but we'll see what that looks like in the next chapter!

We can extend this Model class with our custom data types:

```
namespace App\Models;

use Framework\Database\Model;

class Product extends Model
{
}
```

This is from app/Models/Product.php.

Now, we can get access to the default database connection, using the following code:

```
(new Product())->getConnection()
```

Next, we need to figure out which database table should be used for the Product model. We could infer the table name from the name of the class, but I think we can be explicit about it:

```
protected string $table;

public function setTable(string $table): static
{
    $this->table = $table;
    return $this;
}

public function getTable(): string
{
    if (!isset($this->table)) {
        throw new Exception('$table is not set and getTable is not
        defined');
    }

    return $this->table;
}
```

This is from framework/Database/Model.php.

I think it's better to be explicit about the table name because it makes the system more flexible over all – since it's easier to override an explicit table name. It also leads to less confusion and errors by automation (like odd singular to plural conversion cases).

This means our Product class can either override the getTable method (if it needs to dynamically determine a table name) or define a $table property:

```php
namespace App\Models;

use Framework\Database\Model;

class Product extends Model
{
    protected string $table = 'products';
}
```

This is from app/Models/Product.php.

Let's also make a way for a Model to be hydrated with an array of properties:

```php
protected array $attributes;

public static function with(array $attributes = []): static
{
    $model = new static();
    $model->attributes = $attributes;

    return $model;
}
```

This is from framework/Database/Model.php.

Tying into the Query Builder

Now, we can load one or more rows into these database objects. We're using the 005_ CreateProductsTable.php migration I created between chapters and the three rows I inserted into that table:

```php
public function all(): array
{
    if (!isset($this->type)) {
        $this->select();
    }

    // ...
}

public function first(): array
{
    if (!isset($this->type)) {
        $this->select();
    }

    // ...
}

public static function query(): mixed
{
    $model = new static();

    return $model->getConnection()->query()
        ->from($model->getTable());
}

public static function __callStatic(string $method, array $parameters =
[]): mixed
{
    return static::query()->$method(...$parameters);
}
```

This is from framework/Database/Model.php.

This __callStatic method means we can call any QueryBuilder method on our Product class, and the method will be forwarded to an instance of the query builder. For example, using the all method implemented between chapters, we can fetch all products:

```
Product::all();
// → [['id' => '1', 'name' => 'Large Rocket', ...], ...]
```

We can even find single rows, using "where" clauses:

```
Product::where('id', 1)->first();
// → ['id' => '1', 'name' => 'Large Rocket', ...]
```

This is great, but it's not giving us the rows as model objects, so we need to figure out how to do that. One way would be to make a subclass of MysqlQueryBuilder and SqliteQueryBuilder for each of our data types and override newQuery in each of our custom model types.

That sounds like a lot of awful work to me. We can, instead, define a decorator class that can package up our rows:

```php
namespace Framework\Database;

use Framework\Database\QueryBuilder\QueryBuilder;

class ModelCollector
{
    private QueryBuilder $builder;
    private string $class;

    public function __construct(QueryBuilder $builder, string $class)
    {
        $this->builder = $builder;
        $this->class = $class;
    }

    public function __call(string $method, array $parameters = []): mixed
    {
        $result = $this->builder->$method(...$parameters);
```

```php
        // in case it's a fluent method...
        if ($result instanceof QueryBuilder) {
            $this->builder = $result;
            return $this;
        }

        return $result;
    }

    public function first()
    {
        $class = $this->class;

        $row = $this->builder->first();

        if (!is_null($row)) {
            $row = $class::with($row);
        }

        return $row;
    }

    public function all()
    {
        $class = $this->class;

        $rows = $this->builder->all();

        foreach ($rows as $i => $row) {
            $rows[$i] = $class::with($row);
        }

        return $rows;
    }
}
```

This is from framework/Database/ModelCollector.php.

This decorator takes an instance of the `QueryBuilder` and a model's class name, so that it can intercept all calls to `first` and `all` methods and return the hydrated models each time. We need to use this "collector" when we create new queries:

```php
public static function query(): ModelCollector|QueryBuilder
{
    $model = new static();
    $query = $model->getConnection()->query();

    return (new ModelCollector($query, static::class))
        ->from($model->getTable());
}
```

This is from `framework/Database/Model.php`.

When we query product rows, they'll now be `Product` instances instead of arrays:

```php
Product::all();
// → [object(App\Models\Product), ...]

Product::where('id', 1)->first();
// → object(App\Models\Product)
```

Getters and Setters

This is much better than working with plain old arrays. We've introduced a new problem, which is that we can't easily get at the row attributes anymore. We need to create a common getter method, so that the attributes can be accessed using object lookup syntax:

```php
public function __get(string $property): mixed
{
    if (isset($this->attributes[$property])) {
        return $this->attributes[$property];
    }

    return null;
}
```

```php
public function __set(string $property, $value)
{
    $this->attributes[$property] = $value;
}
```

This is from `framework/Database/Model.php`.

You might want to take this a step further and throw exceptions when the __get method tries to find properties that don't exist on the database row or when the __set method tries to set the value of an unknown row. I think, to do it properly, we'd need to store the original column names of the database row or have a list of known columns in each model class...

Given these __set and __get methods, we can now access attributes using object lookup syntax:

```php
Product::where('id', 1)->first()->name;
// → 'Large Rocket'
```

What about if we want to allow `Product` to define custom getters and setters? Let's define a name getter that starts each word with an uppercase letter and a `description` setter that limits the number of description characters to 50:

```php
protected function setDescriptionAttribute(string $value)
{
    $limit = 50;
    $ending = '...';

    if (mb_strwidth($value, 'UTF-8') <= $limit) {
        return $value;
    }

    return rtrim(mb_strimwidth($value, 0, $limit, '', 'UTF-8')) . $ending;
}
```

This is from `app/Models/Product.php`.

It's a bit safer suffixing these methods with `Attribute`, since we dynamically compose their names in the following code snippets. "Attribute" relates to the internal name of the array of database row attributes.

We need to figure out if these methods should be called, based on the name of the property that is being accessed:

```php
public function __get(string $property): mixed
{
    $getter = 'get' . ucfirst($property) . 'Attribute';

    if (method_exists($this, $getter)) {
        return $this->$getter($this->attributes[$property] ?? null);
    }

    if (isset($this->attributes[$property])) {
        return $this->attributes[$property];
    }

    return null;
}

public function __set(string $property, $value)
{
    $setter = 'set' . ucfirst($property) . 'Attribute';

    if (method_exists($this, $setter)) {
        $this->attributes[$property] = $this->$setter($value);
    }

    $this->attributes[$property] = $value;
}
```

This is from `framework/Database/Model.php`.

These magic methods check for the existence of methods named `get*Attribute` and `set*Attribute`, calling out to those instead. If we wanted, we could still access `$this->attributes` inside our getters and setters, but most of the time we'd only need the one value being set or looked up.

Inserting, Updating, and Deleting

The easiest way to tell if we need to insert or update is by checking for the existence of an id attribute. We do need to add an update and delete method to the QueryBuilder though. Let's begin with the update method:

```php
public function prepare(): PdoStatement
{
    // ...

    if ($this->type === 'update') {
        $query = $this->compileUpdate($query);
        $query = $this->compileWheres($query);
    }

    // ...
}

protected function compileUpdate(string $query): string
{
    $joinedColumns = '';

    foreach ($this->columns as $i => $column) {
        if ($i > 0) {
            $joinedColumns .= ', ';
        }

        $joinedColumns = " {$column} = :{$column}";
    }

    $query .= " UPDATE {$this->table} SET {$joinedColumns}";

    return $query;
}

public function update(array $columns, array $values): int
{
    $this->type = 'update';
    $this->columns = $columns;
    $this->values = $values;
```

```
$statement = $this->prepare();

return $statement->execute($this->getWhereValues() + $values);
}
```

This is from `framework/Database/QueryBuilder/QueryBuilder.php`.

We're following a similar pattern to the code we used for "where" and "insert" clauses, including the placeholders for values in prepared statements.

SQL "update" clauses have a slightly different syntax to insert statements:

UPDATE products **SET** field = :field **WHERE id** = :id

Some engines support an alternative syntax that more closely mirrors the syntax of "insert" clauses, but it isn't as portable across engines as this standard version.

Using this new update method, we can update the Model class to have a universal save method:

```
protected array $dirty = [];

public function __set(string $property, $value)
{
    $setter = 'set' . ucfirst($property) . 'Attribute';

    array_push($this->dirty, $property);

    // ...
}

public function save(): static
{
    $values = [];

    foreach ($this->dirty as $dirty) {
        $values[$dirty] = $this->attributes[$dirty];
    }

    $data = [array_keys($values), $values];

    $query = static::query();
```

```
    if (isset($this->attributes['id'])) {
        $query
            ->where('id', $this->attributes['id'])
            ->update(...$data);

        return $this;
    }

    $query->insert(...$data);

    $this->attributes['id'] = $query->getLastInsertId();
    $this->dirty = [];

    return $this;
}
```

This is from `framework/Database/Model.php`.

If we passed the full $attributes property to the update and insert methods, we might be saving fields that have not changed.

Instead, we can use the $dirty array to store the names of fields that have changed. This means we will only send the data for fields that have been set or changed.

We need to make sure that we're storing the ID of a newly created row back into the model object, so that subsequent calls to the save method perform an update instead of an insert.

To do this, we need to add a method for returning the previously inserted row to the QueryBuilder class:

```
public function getLastInsertId(): string
{
    return $this->connection->pdo()->lastInsertId();
}
```

This is from `framework/Database/QueryBuilder/QueryBuilder.php`.

We can use this to get and store the ID for a newly created row:

```
public function save(): static
{
    // ...

    $query->insert(...$data);

    $this->attributes['id'] = $query->getLastInsertId();

    return $this;
}
```

This is from `framework/Database/Model.php`.

This code works like a charm! We can create or update rows using very similar code (and not care about what SQL query is being used underneath):

```
$product = Product::where('id', 1)->first();
$product->description = 'This is a new, better description';
$product->save();
// → updated existing database row

$product = new Product();
$product->name = 'A whole new product';
$product->description = 'The best description in the world';
$product->save();
// → created new database row and set $product->id
```

Now, let's focus our attention on deleting rows from the database. We need a couple new methods: one on `QueryBuilder` and another on `Model`:

```
public function prepare(): PdoStatement
{
    // ...

    if ($this->type === 'delete') {
        $query = $this->compileDelete($query);
        $query = $this->compileWheres($query);
    }
```

```
    // ...
}

protected function compileDelete(string $query): string
{
    $query .= " DELETE FROM {$this->table}";
    return $query;
}

public function delete(): int
{
    $this->type = 'delete';

    $statement = $this->prepare();

    return $statement->execute($this->getWhereValues());
}
```

This is from framework/Database/QueryBuilder/QueryBuilder.php.

"Delete" clauses require no data or columns. They don't even require "where" clauses, but it's unwise to use them without one. That's ok, though, because the Model-> delete method will always define one (or no-op):

```
public function delete(): static
{
    if (isset($this->attributes['id'])) {
        static::query()
            ->where('id', $this->attributes['id'])
            ->delete();
    }

    return $this;
}
```

This is from framework/Database/Model.php.

It's equally valid to throw an exception if a row is being deleted before it has been saved, but we should at least make sure we're not sending an unconstrained "delete" clause to the database.

Our implementation doesn't deal well with the situation in which the `delete` method is called and then the `save` method is called. We probably want to make "save" a no-op or throw an exception to say that a deleted model can't be saved again.

Casting Values

Most database engines give back the data in a string format. Let's add some code to cast values to the appropriate type for each column. We can do this in the `Model` class:

```php
public function __get(string $property): mixed
{
    $getter = 'get' . ucfirst($property) . 'Attribute';

    $value = null;

    if (method_exists($this, $getter)) {
        $value = $this->$getter($this->attributes[$property] ?? null);
    }

    if (isset($this->attributes[$property])) {
        $value = $this->attributes[$property];
    }

    if (isset($this->casts[$property]) && is_callable($this->casts[$property])) {
        $value = $this->casts[$property]($value);
    }

    return $value;
}
```

This is from `framework/Database/Model.php`.

We've switched things around so that whatever value we get can be passed through a callable thing, set in the $casts property. It's a little easier to explain with an example. Say we wanted to cast a product's ID value to an integer; we can define a callable function and set it on that $casts property:

```php
namespace App\Models;

use Framework\Database\Model;

function toInt($value): int
{
    return (int) $value;
}

class Product extends Model
{
    protected array $casts = [
        'id' => 'App\Models\toInt',
    ];

    // ...
}
```

This is from app/Models/Product.php.

The value of the ID attribute will be passed through this toInt function before being returned with object access ($obj->id). We can define cast functions in the framework helpers or even extend this code to recognize and use classes instead of functions. I think this is good enough for now, though...

Relationships

The final bit of code I want to tackle is to manage simple relationships. Consider the following example:

```php
$user = new User();
$user->email = "cgpitt@gmail.com";
$user->save();
```

```
$profile = new Profile();
$profile->user_id = $user->id;
$profile->save();

$user->profile;
// → object(App\Models\Profile)
```

I want to make that kind of code work. It represents the "has one" type of relationship, because a user "has one" profile.

Let's define a method on Model that we can use to indicate this kind of relationship and then see how the method can be used:

```
public function hasOne(string $class, string $foreignKey, string
$primaryKey = 'id'): mixed
{
    $model = new $class;
    $query = $class::query()->from($model->getTable())->where($foreignKey,
    $this->attributes['id']);

    return new Relationship($query, 'first');
}
```

This is from framework/Database/Model.php.

One simple way to represent relationships is as partially complete queries. Here, we're starting to build a query about the related data. The Relationship class looks like this:

```
namespace Framework\Database;

use Framework\Database\ModelCollector;

class Relationship
{
    public ModelCollector $collector;
    public string $method;
```

```php
    public function __construct(ModelCollector $collector, string $method)
    {
        $this->collector = $collector;
        $this->method = $method;
    }

    public function __invoke(array $parameters = []): mixed
    {
        return $this->collector->$method(...$parameters);
    }

    public function __call(string $method, array $parameters = []): mixed
    {
        return $this->collector->$method(...$parameters);
    }
}
```

This is from framework/Database/Relationship.php.

It's just a decorator. All method calls are passed to the underlying ModelCollector instance – which is what the static query method returns – and a relationship instance can also be called like a function. This means we can use the relationship in the following ways:

```php
$user = new User();
$user->email = 'cgpitt@gmail.com';
$user->save();

$profile = new Profile();
$profile->user_id = $user->id;
$profile->save();

$user->profile()->first();
// → object(App\Models\Profile)

// or
```

```
$relationship = $user->profile();
$relationship()->first();
// → object(App\Models\Profile)
```

We store the additional $method property because it tells us how to resolve the query if used with object access. Let me show you what I mean. Let's modify the Model->__get method:

```php
public function __get(string $property): mixed
{
    $getter = 'get' . ucfirst($property) . 'Attribute';

    $value = null;

    if (method_exists($this, $property)) {
        $relationship = $this->$property();
        $method = $relationship->method;

        $value = $relationship->$method();
    }

    // ...
}
```

This is from framework/Database/Model.php.

This means we can now access the related model with the following code:

```php
$user = new User();
$user->email = 'cgpitt@gmail.com';
$user->save();

$profile = new Profile();
$profile->user_id = $user->id;
$profile->save();

$user->profile;
// → object(App\Models\Profile)
```

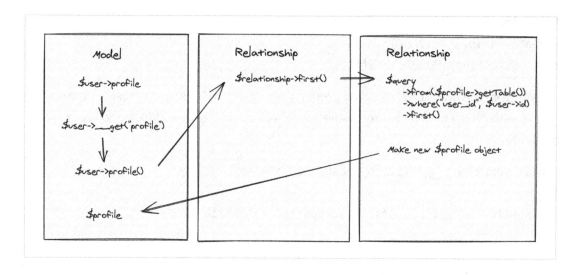

Relationship call graph

Let's extend these relationships to represent "has many" and "belongs to" relationship types:

```php
public function hasMany(string $class, string $foreignKey, string
$primaryKey = 'id'): mixed
{
    $model = new $class;
    $query = $class::query()->from($model->getTable())->where($foreignKey,
    $this->attributes['id']);

    return new Relationship($query, 'all');
}

public function belongsTo(string $class, string $foreignKey, string
$primaryKey = 'id'): mixed
{
    $model = new $class;
    $query = $class::query()->from($model->getTable())->where($primaryKey,
    $this->attributes[$foreignKey]);

    return new Relationship($query, 'first');
}
```

This is from framework/Database/Model.php.

These methods can be used to define the new relationship types, in their respective models:

```php
namespace App\Models;

use Framework\Database\Model;

class Order extends Model
{
    protected string $table = 'orders';

    public function user(): mixed
    {
        return $this->belongsTo(User::class, 'user_id');
    }
}
```

This is from app/Models/Order.php.

```php
namespace App\Models;

use Framework\Database\Model;

class Profile extends Model
{
    protected string $table = 'profiles';

    public function user(): mixed
    {
        return $this->belongsTo(User::class, 'user_id');
    }
}
```

This is from app/Models/Product.php.

```php
namespace App\Models;

use Framework\Database\Model;

class User extends Model
{
    protected string $table = 'users';

    public function profile(): mixed
    {
        return $this->hasOne(Profile::class, 'user_id');
    }

    public function orders(): mixed
    {
        return $this->hasMany(Order::class, 'user_id');
    }
}
```

This is from app/Models/User.php.

I think it's wild that we've been able to represent these relationships with so few adjustments to our existing Model and QueryBuilder classes.

What About Attributes

One of the fascinating additions to PHP 8.0 is the ability to define and use attributes. They look a bit like comments (and will therefore be ignored by older versions of PHP), but they can be accessed via a different sort of reflection.

Imagine we wanted to allow users to define the table for their model as an attribute, perhaps using code resembling this:

```php
#[Table('users')]
class User extends Model
{
    public function profile(): mixed
```

```
    {
        return $this->hasOne(Profile::class, 'user_id');
    }

    public function orders(): mixed
    {
        return $this->hasMany(Order::class, 'user_id');
    }
}
```

We could actually reach into the attributes for this class and get the table name from there. Let's try that in the Model class:

```
public function getTable(): string
{
    if (!isset($this->table)) {
        $reflector = new ReflectionClass(static::class);

        foreach ($reflector->getAttributes() as $attribute) {
            if ($attribute->getName() == TableName::class) {
                return $attribute->getArguments()[0];
            }
        }

        throw new Exception('$table is not set and getTable is not
        defined');
    }

    return $this->table;
}
```

This is from framework/Database/Model.php.

We'll also need to define this attribute – as all attributes need to be defined as classes:

```php
namespace Framework\Database;

#[Attribute]
class TableName
{
    public string $name;

    public function __construct(string $name)
    {
        $this->name = $name;
    }
}
```

This is from `framework/Database/TableName.php`.

I think this is an interesting use of attributes, but be careful not to go overboard with attributes as it can lead to a lot of searching, when folks want to know what the attributes are doing under the hood.

With method overrides (which is the approach we used for the `getTable`), it's very clear how and where the table name is being generated. Not so much with the attribute format.

I don't want it to seem like I don't like attributes. I think this same problem (of overuse) can apply to magic methods. We may even have crossed that line with the magic methods in this ORM code.

I think a good measure of use for attributes and magic methods is whether they can be used while still maintaining a flexible and easy-to-understand system. When code is harder to change or understand, it's a sign that we should review and refactor our code to use less magic.

Caveats

Here are some more challenges for you to overcome in your framework and application:

1. We're currently hard-coding the `id` column name in a few places. It would be cooler if this was something we could override…

2. We're still using the old `QueryBuilder` code in the controllers.

3. We could be doing a lot more type-checking around things like `$this->attributes['id']`, to make sure we're dealing with numeric IDs.

4. I think we're using `mixed` too much. What about defining the return types better, perhaps even through union types?

I'll address some of these things between this chapter and the next, so be sure to try your hand at any that interest you before reading the next chapter.

How the Pros Do It

The ORM code in this chapter is heavily inspired by the developer experience of Laravel's ORM. It's not as feature-rich as Eloquent and does a few small things differently (like how the casting is handled and relationships are defined), but it'll feel familiar to a Laravel developer.

Laravel has a much wider set of relationships you can define, like "belongs to many" and "polymorphic" relationships. I think they're great features, but they'll probably take another 20 pages to achieve in this chapter.

Eloquent doesn't use attributes, nor does it use the previous widely used form of attributes – phpDoc comments. Most configuration is done through properties and overrides, as demonstrated in this chapter.

Eloquent and the Laravel database library are closely entwined, and the database library is fantastically rich in features. The docs on where clauses, for example, are massive.

Eloquent reuses this underlying database functionality with the Eloquent query building (in a similar way to how we did it in this chapter), but all the added functionality of the database library is available on Eloquent models.

Eloquent also provides features called eager loading and lazy loading. These circumvent a problem in the ORM we've built, called the N+1 problem.

Without going into too much detail, the approach we've followed might lead to a large number of queries when fetching related records. Eager loading prevents this by performing as few queries as possible and linking related records up in memory.

Lazy loading does as much of the work (of querying from the database) as possible, only when needed.

Doctrine ORM

Doctrine is the organization of a collection of libraries, the most popular being Doctrine ORM. Doctrine also has a database library, on top of which the ORM is built.

The main differences between Doctrine ORM and Eloquent are that Doctrine favors an approach called entity management and that Doctrine favors configuration over convention.

Entity management is the process through which objects are persisted to the database all at once and not by their own logic. Perhaps I can better illustrate the difference using some pseudo-code:

```
// in eloquent
$product = new Product();
$product->name = 'ACME product';
$product->save();

// in doctrine orm
$product = new Product();
$product->name = 'ACME product';

$manager = new EntityManager();
$manager->persist($product);
$manager->flush();
```

Eloquent favors convention over configuration, so there's far less to set up before you get started, but there are also a lot of assumptions floating around about how you want your data to look and your logic to work.

In fact, Eloquent models look very different from Doctrine models. There's almost no magic in Doctrine models, whereas Eloquent models are quite magical.

Summary

This has been a rewarding deep dive into the process of building an ORM. I hope you found it as exciting as I did. It's probably the most complex topic we're going to cover in this book, so don't feel bad if you need to take extra time to get a handle on the things we covered.

In the next chapter, we're going to solve the problem of boilerplate, as we build our own service locator.

CHAPTER 8

Building a Dependency Injection Container

In the previous chapter, we built a really awesome ORM. With it, we can take our database work to a whole new level. It should give you lots to tinker with and think about.

In this chapter, we're going to work on eliminating boilerplate and making it easier to share dependencies between different parts of our system.

During the Break…

Before we dive into building a dependency injection container, we're going to review a few improvements I made to the website between chapters.

The biggest change was to switch the database library code out for the ORM code. This is what the previous version looked like:

```
$factory = new Factory();

$factory->addConnector('mysql', function($config) {
    return new MysqlConnection($config);
});

$factory->addConnector('sqlite', function($config) {
    return new SqliteConnection($config);
});

$config = require __DIR__ . '/../../../config/database.php';

$connection = $factory->connect($config[$config['default']]);
```

© Christopher Pitt 2021
C. Pitt, *Pro PHP 8 MVC*, https://doi.org/10.1007/978-1-4842-6957-2_8

```
$products = $connection
    ->query()
    ->select()
    ->from('products')
    ->all();

$productsWithRoutes = array_map(fn($product) => array_merge($product, [
    'route' => $this->router->route('view-product', ['product' =>
    $product['id']]]),
]), $products);
```

This is from app/Http/Controllers/ShowHomePageController.php.

And this is what the new version looks like:

```
$products = Product::all();

$productsWithRoutes = array_map(function($product) {
    $product->route = $this->router->route('view-product', ['product' =>
    $product->id]);
    return $product;
}, $products);
```

This is from app/Http/Controllers/ShowHomePageController.php.

Admittedly, much of this is a reduction in the boilerplate code for establishing new database connections. That code has moved to the Model class, but it's going to move in this chapter again.

This change to models meant using object access in the templates:

```
@extends('layout') @includes('includes/large-feature') @foreach($products
as $i
=> $product)
<div
  class="
        z-10
```

```
        @if($i % 2 === 0)
            bg-gray-50
        @endif
    "
>
  <div class="container mx-auto px-8 py-8 md:py-16">
    <h2 class="text-3xl font-bold">{{ $product->name }}</h2>
    <p class="text-xl my-4">{!! $product->description !!}</p>
    <a
      href="{{ $product->route }}"
      class="bg-indigo-500 rounded-lg p-2 text-white"
    >
      Order
    </a>
  </div>
</div>
@endforeach
```

This is from `resources/views/home.advanced.php`.

On the product view page, we need to get a single product, based on route parameters. I added a method to the Model class to do this quicker:

```
public static function find(int $id): static
{
    return static::where('id', $id)->first();
}
```

This is from `framework/Database/Model.php`.

This makes that controller look like this:

```php
public function handle()
{
    $parameters = $this->router->current()->parameters();

    $product = Product::find((int) $parameters['product']);

    return view('products/view', [
        'product' => $product,
        'orderAction' => $this->router->route('order-product', ['product'
        => $product->id]),
        'csrf' => csrf(),
    ]);
}
```

This is from app/Http/Controllers/Products/ShowProductController.php.

---

find is super helpful and quite a common operation in applications that involve databases.

Lastly, I thought it would be cool for people to be able to register new accounts and use those accounts to log in. User registration is essential for commerce applications.

This is what the registration and login controllers look like:

```php
public function handle()
{
    // check the csrf token...
    secure();

    $data = validate($_POST, [
        'name' => ['required'],
        'email' => ['required', 'email'],
        'password' => ['required', 'min:10'],
    ], 'register_errors');

    $user = new User();
    $user->name = $data['name'];
```

```php
$user->email = $data['email'];
$user->password = password_hash($data['password'], PASSWORD_DEFAULT);
$user->save();

// store a variable to show a message to the user...
$_SESSION['registered'] = true;

return redirect($this->router->route('show-home-page'));
}
```

This is from app/Http/Controllers/Users/RegisterUserController.php.

---

password_hash is a relatively new addition to PHP. It provides a convenient way to generate cryptographically strong passwords. The Bcrypt provider generates a salt and adds it to the hash.

Since we only store the hash, we need to use another built-in function to verify that the password is correct:

```php
public function handle()
{
    // check the csrf token...
    secure();

    $data = validate($_POST, [
        'email' => ['required', 'email'],
        'password' => ['required', 'min:10'],
    ], 'login_errors');

    $user = User::where('email', $data['email'])->first();

    if ($user && password_verify($data['password'], $user->password)) {
        $_SESSION['user_id'] = $user->id;
    }

    return redirect($this->router->route('show-home-page'));
}
```

This is from `app/Http/Controllers/Users/LogInUserController.php`.

I stopped short of messaging login/register/logout successes or failures, but feel free to pick that up if you're keen. This wraps up the auth work, so it's time to jump into dependency injection and service location.

What Is a Dependency Injection Container Used For?

As we've seen, there's a lot of boilerplate involved in stitching together a large application and custom framework. The helpers are an example of this:

```php
function view(string $template, array $data = []): View\View
{
    static $manager;

    if (!$manager) {
        $manager = new View\Manager();

        // ...lots of manager setup
    }

    return $manager->resolve($template, $data);
}
```

This is from `framework/helpers.php`.

We have a couple helpers – just like this – where we create and configure new managers. The setup is required, but it shouldn't live inside these functions. It's not easy to customize the configuration, and it's probably tricky to test.

Another example of problematic boilerplate can be found in `Model`:

```php
public function getConnection(): Connection
{
    if (!isset($this->connection)) {
        $factory = new Factory();
```

```
$factory->addConnector('mysql', function($config) {
    return new MysqlConnection($config);
});

$factory->addConnector('sqlite', function($config) {
    return new SqliteConnection($config);
});

$config = require basePath() . 'config/database.php';

$this->connection = $factory->connect($config[$config['default']]);
    }

    return $this->connection;
}
```

This is from `framework/Database/Model.php`.

At least it's easier to override the connection if setConnection is called before getConnection or if getConnection is overridden in a subclass.

A more subtle example is in the routes file:

```
$router->add(
    'GET', '/',
    [new ShowHomePageController($router), 'handle'],
)->name('show-home-page');
```

This is from `app/routes.php`.

We need to generate routes in the ShowHomePageController class, so we pass an instance of the router to it. What if we needed access to something else? In a few chapters, we're going to be building up session, cache, and logging. Those aren't things we'd want to create new instances of every time we used them.

Wouldn't it be cooler if we could type-hint method parameters and have those parameters automatically resolved? Imagine something like this:

```php
public function handle(Request $request, Router $router, Session $session)
{
    secure();

    $data = $request->validate([
        'email' => ['required', 'email'],
        'password' => ['required', 'min:10'],
    ], 'login_errors');

    $user = User::where('email', $data['email'])->first();

    if ($user && password_verify($data['password'], $user->password)) {
        $session->put('user_id', $user->id);
    }

    return redirect($router->route('show-home-page'));
}
```

It's not that I dislike helper functions, but they really should be more concise, and it should be effortless to customize what they use and return.

Here are some features I want our dependency injection container to have:

1. A way to store (or bind) dependency instances

2. A way to retrieve (or resolve) those dependency instances

3. A way to proxy function or method calls so that type-hinted parameters can be resolved out of the container

4. Some structure for how to configure the container

The container is the core of the framework, but we need to separate the dependency injection side of things from the configuration and loading side of things.

Container and App structure

It'll become clearer why this kind of design works as we go along.

Let's Get Building!

The first two requirements are similar to code we've written before. We can create a couple of arrays: one to store factory functions and another to store the things these factory functions create:

```php
namespace Framework;

use InvalidArgumentException;

class Container
{
    private array $bindings = [];
    private array $resolved = [];

    public function bind(string $alias, callable $factory): static
    {
        $this->bindings[$alias] = $factory;
        $this->resolved[$alias] = null;

        return $this;
    }

    public function resolve(string $alias): mixed
    {
        if (!isset($this->bindings[$alias])) {
            throw new InvalidArgumentException("{$alias} is not bound");
        }

        if (!isset($this->resolved[$alias])) {
            $this->resolved[$alias] = call_user_func($this->bindings[$alias], $this);
        }
```

```
        return $this->resolved[$alias];
    }
}
```

This is from `framework/Container.php;`.

I want us to be able to use this as quickly as possible, so let's create the App subclass and move most of `public/index.php` into it. We're using the container as a central store, so we need to make it a singleton.

Making the container a singleton isn't strictly required if we're super careful to only create it in one place. Forcing it to be used as a singleton makes sure that it will always be the same instance we're referring to, no matter how many times we try to "create" it.

```php
namespace Framework;

use Dotenv\Dotenv;
use Framework\Routing\Router;

class App extends Container
{
    private static $instance;

    public static function getInstance()
    {
        if (!static::$instance) {
            static::$instance = new static();
        }

        return static::$instance;
    }

    private function __construct() {}
    private function __clone() {}
```

```php
    public function run()
    {
        session_start();

        $dotenv = Dotenv::createImmutable(__DIR__ . '/..');
        $dotenv->load();

        $router = new Router();

        $routes = include __DIR__ . '/../app/routes.php';
        $routes($router);

        print $router->dispatch();
    }
}
```

This is from `framework/App.php`.

This means we can cut a bunch of code out of `public/index.php`. Here's what that looks like, after commenting out the existing code and calling the new method:

```php
require_once __DIR__ . '/../vendor/autoload.php';

// basePath(__DIR__ . '/../');

// session_start();

// $dotenv = Dotenv\Dotenv::createImmutable(__DIR__ . '/..');
// $dotenv->load();

// $router = new Framework\Routing\Router();

// $routes = require_once __DIR__ . '/../app/routes.php';
// $routes($router);

// print $router->dispatch();

$app = \Framework\App::getInstance();
$app->bind('paths.base', fn() => __DIR__ . '/../');
$app->run();
```

This is from public/index.php.

Finally, until we have a neat way to pass $app around to other classes, we should implement singleton methods and a helper to use them:

```
use Framework\App;

if (!function_exists('basePath')) {
    function basePath(string $newBasePath = null): ?string
    {
        // static $basePath;

        // if (!is_null($newBasePath)) {
        //     $basePath = $newBasePath;
        // }

        // return $basePath;

        return app('paths.base');
    }
}

if (!function_exists('app')) {
    function app(string $alias = null): mixed
    {
        if (is_null($alias)) {
            return App::getInstance();
        }

        return App::getInstance()->resolve($alias);
    }
}
```

This is from framework/helpers.php.

Binding and Resolving

The best way to make sure that this works is to refactor the other helper functions to use the container, instead of static variables. Let's change the view and validate helpers to use the app helper function:

```php
if (!function_exists('view')) {
    app()->bind('view', function($app) {
        $manager = new View\Manager();

        $manager->addPath(__DIR__ . '/../resources/views');
        $manager->addPath(__DIR__ . '/../resources/images');

        $manager->addEngine('basic.php', new View\Engine\BasicEngine());
        $manager->addEngine('advanced.php', new View\Engine\
        AdvancedEngine());
        $manager->addEngine('php', new View\Engine\PhpEngine());
        $manager->addEngine('svg', new View\Engine\LiteralEngine());

        $manager->addMacro('escape', fn($value) => htmlspecialchars($value,
        ENT_QUOTES));
        $manager->addMacro('includes', fn(...$params) => print
        view(...$params));

        return $manager;
    });

    function view(string $template, array $data = []): View\View
    {
        return app()->resolve('view')->resolve($template, $data);
    }
}

if (!function_exists('validate')) {
    app()->bind('validator', function($app) {
        $manager = new Validation\Manager();

        $manager->addRule('required', new Validation\Rule\RequiredRule());
        $manager->addRule('email', new Validation\Rule\EmailRule());
        $manager->addRule('min', new Validation\Rule\MinRule());
```

```php
        return $manager;
    });

    function validate(array $data, array $rules, string $sessionName =
    'errors')
    {
        return app('validator')->validate($data, $rules, $sessionName);
    }
}
```

This is from `framework/helpers.php`.

This puts bind, resolve, and app to the test. Both view and validate are reduced to a single line of code, which is good because the configuration of these dependencies should not take place inside these methods.

I hate that the calls to app()->bind(...) are sitting inside this helpers file, though. Let's move the view configuration into a configuration class.

We're going to put it in a new kind of class, called a "provider," which is what the framework will use to "load" commonly used code. This is the first of many providers we're going to make:

```php
namespace Framework\Provider;

use Framework\App;
use Framework\View\Manager;
use Framework\View\Engine\BasicEngine;
use Framework\View\Engine\AdvancedEngine;
use Framework\View\Engine\PhpEngine;
use Framework\View\Engine\LiteralEngine;

class ViewProvider
{
    public function bind(App $app)
    {
        $app->bind('view', function($app) {
            $manager = new Manager();
```

```php
        $this->bindPaths($app, $manager);
        $this->bindMacros($app, $manager);
        $this->bindEngines($app, $manager);

        return $manager;
    });
}

private function bindPaths(App $app, Manager $manager)
{
    $manager->addPath($app->resolve('paths.base') . '/resources/
    views');
    $manager->addPath($app->resolve('paths.base') . '/resources/
    images');
}

private function bindMacros(App $app, Manager $manager)
{
    $manager->addMacro('escape', fn($value) => htmlspecialchars($value,
    ENT_QUOTES));
    $manager->addMacro('includes', fn(...$params) => print
    view(...$params));
}

private function bindEngines(App $app, Manager $manager)
{
    $app->bind('view.engine.basic', fn() => new BasicEngine());
    $app->bind('view.engine.advanced', fn() => new AdvancedEngine());
    $app->bind('view.engine.php', fn() => new PhpEngine());
    $app->bind('view.engine.literal', fn() => new LiteralEngine());

    $manager->addEngine('basic.php', $app->resolve('view.engine.basic'));
    $manager->addEngine('advanced.php', $app->resolve('view.engine.
    advanced'));
    $manager->addEngine('php', $app->resolve('view.engine.php'));
    $manager->addEngine('svg', $app->resolve('view.engine.literal'));
}
}
```

This is from `framework/Provider/ViewProvider.php`.

This is much the same, with the exception that we're also making the view engines available in case they need to be reused. Let's also add a new configuration file to list the providers that we want loaded by the framework:

```
return [
    \Framework\Provider\ViewProvider::class,
];
```

This is from `config/providers.php`.

We can use this config file, in the App class, to load providers and execute their `bind` functions. We may want to hook into other parts of the app inside these providers, so let's make the `bind` method optional:

```
public function run()
{
    session_start();

    $basePath = $this->resolve('paths.base');

    $this->configure($basePath);
    $this->bindProviders($basePath);
    $this->dispatch($basePath);
}

private function configure(string $basePath)
{
    $dotenv = Dotenv::createImmutable($basePath);
    $dotenv->load();
}

private function bindProviders(string $basePath)
{
    $providers = require "{$basePath}/config/providers.php";
```

```
        foreach ($providers as $provider) {
            $instance = new $provider;

            if (method_exists($instance, 'bind')) {
                $instance->bind($this);
            }
        }
    }
}

private function dispatch(string $basePath)
{
    $router = new Router();

    $this->bind(Router::class, fn() => $router);

    $routes = require "{$basePath}/app/routes.php";
    $routes($router);

    print $router->dispatch();
}
```

This is from `framework/App.php`.

Now, we can comment out all of the configuration from before the view helper, and views will still be rendered:

```
if (!function_exists('view')) {
    // app()->bind('view', function($app) {
    //     $manager = new View\Manager();

    //     $manager->addPath(__DIR__ . '/../resources/views');
    //     $manager->addPath(__DIR__ . '/../resources/images');

    //     $manager->addEngine('basic.php', new View\Engine\BasicEngine());
    //     $manager->addEngine('advanced.php', new View\Engine\
    //         AdvancedEngine());
    //     $manager->addEngine('php', new View\Engine\PhpEngine());
    //     $manager->addEngine('svg', new View\Engine\LiteralEngine());
```

```
//      $manager->addMacro('escape', fn($value) =>
        htmlspecialchars($value, ENT_QUOTES));
//      $manager->addMacro('includes', fn(...$params) => print
        view(...$params));

//      return $manager;
// });

function view(string $template, array $data = []): View\View
{
    return app()->resolve('view')->resolve($template, $data);
}
}
```

This is from `framework/helpers.php`.

Moving this configuration is one of the most gratifying things I've done in this application. Take some time to migrate the configuration of the validator to its own new provider class, to get the hang of this style of configuration.

Resolving Function Parameters

The only other feature we're going to implement, right now, is the ability to call a function or method and have missing parameters resolved from the container. We're going to have to use some reflection to figure this out, starting with the parameters the function expects:

```
public function call(array|callable $callable, array $parameters = []):
mixed
{
    $reflector = $this->getReflector($callable);

    $dependencies = [];

    foreach ($reflector->getParameters() as $parameter) {
        $name = $parameter->getName();
        $type = $parameter->getType();
```

```
        // ...do something with name and type
    }
}

private function getReflector(array|callable $callable): ReflectionMethod|R
eflectionFunction
{
    if (is_array($callable)) {
        return new ReflectionMethod($callable[0], $callable[1]);
    }

    return new ReflectionFunction($callable);
}
```

This is from framework/App.php.

ReflectionFunction and ReflectionMethod have this handy getParameters
method, which returns ReflectionParameter objects, for each parameter defined in the
function or method.

In order to get those, we need to pick between a callable (function or string or
Closure) and an array. The only reason for it to be an array is if we're referring to a
method on a class or object.

Given the name and type, we can actually tell if the parameters have been provided
or if they need to be resolved from the container:

```
foreach ($reflector->getParameters() as $parameter) {
    $name = $parameter->getName();
    $type = $parameter->getType();

    if (isset($parameters[$name])) {
        $dependencies[$name] = $parameters[$name];
        continue;
    }

    if ($parameter->isDefaultValueAvailable()) {
        $dependencies[$name] = $parameter->getDefaultValue();
        continue;
    }
```

```php
    if ($type instanceof ReflectionNamedType) {
        $dependencies[$name] = $this->resolve($type);
        continue;
    }

    throw new InvalidArgumentException("{$name} cannot be resolved");
}
```

This is from `framework/App.php`.

We try to resolve the parameters in the following order:

1. If someone calls app()->call(...) with an array of parameters and the expected method parameter has a matching value in the second call argument, then we just use that.

2. If the method has a default value for that parameter, then that's the value that we use.

3. Finally, if no value has been defined and no default value is present, then we try to resolve the dependency from the container.

These two new methods use union types to define their parameter type hints. It allows us to be specific about types, but also allows for varied usage.

In order to use this with routes, we need to change how they are called by the router:

```php
public function dispatch()
{
    if (is_array($this->handler)) {
        [$class, $method] = $this->handler;

        if (is_string($class)) {
            // return (new $class)->{$method}();
            return app()->call([new $class, $method]);
        }

        // return $class->{$method}();
        return app()->call([$class, $method]);
    }
```

```php
// return call_user_func($this->handler);

    return app()->call($this->handler);
}
```

This is from `framework/Routing/Router.php`.

Now, we can inject any dependencies we need:

```php
// protected Router $router;

// public function __construct(Router $router)
// {
//     $this->router = $router;
// }
public function handle(Router $router)
{
    $products = Product::all();

    $productsWithRoutes = array_map(function ($product) use ($router) {
        $product->route = $router->route('view-product', ['product' =>
        $product->id]);
        return $product;
    }, $products);

    return view('home', [
        'products' => $productsWithRoutes,
    ]);
}
```

This is from `app/Http/Controllers/ShowHomePageController.php`.

Additionally, we can resolve the dependencies of any method we like, by calling it with the call method:

```
use App\Models\Product;
use Framework\View\Manager;

$html = app()->call(
    fn(Manager $view, $product) => $view->resolve('embed', $product),
    ['product' => Product::first()],
);
```

Pretty neat! I think this is going to make a huge difference going forward and gives us a chance to refactor a bunch of our existing code.

Caveats

Here are some things I would consider adding or changing. Have fun trying some of them out:

1. As mentioned, I think it would be cool to make a service provider for the validation code.

2. We could even move other bits of configuration to providers, like the code that starts the session or the code that binds the router to the container.

3. It's possible to replace bound dependencies with newer or decorated ones, but it's not straightforward. Wonder if we could add another container method to extend bindings.

Different Approaches to Explore

We've taken a very opinionated approach to building this service locator and dependency injection container. There are many alternatives to Laravel's container – which is what I've based much of this pattern on – and they're all great.

Here are some things we could consider supporting:

1. A less "magic" approach to picking parameters for method calls

2. Allowing for constructor dependency injection, so that dependencies can be shared between methods instead of being resolved for each "magic" method call

One of the libraries, similar to the one we've made, which I often like to use, is called PHP-DI. It prefers configuration over convention, but it has a similar look and feel to the container library we've made.

Summary

In this chapter, we took a huge step forward in organizing our code. I'm excited for what this means for our framework and website. I'm going to busy myself with some of the challenges set in the preceding...

In the next chapter, we're going to deal with the long-overdue subject of testing. We'll figure out how to begin testing and build up a set of helpers that we can reuse going forward.

CHAPTER 9

Testing Our Framework

In the previous chapter, we built a service locator and dependency injection container, so that we can share parts of our framework without excess boilerplate.

In this chapter, we're going to learn how to test that new code and how to generally structure our application and tests so that they give us the most benefit for the time we put into them.

Between the Chapters...

I want to quickly touch on some of the changes I made since the last chapter. The dependency injection container is a powerful tool because it cuts down on the repetition of code and makes it easier to structure our framework code.

Using the container, I was able to move the validation code to a new provider:

```php
namespace Framework\Provider;

use Framework\App;
use Framework\Validation\Manager;
use Framework\Validation\Rule\RequiredRule;
use Framework\Validation\Rule\EmailRule;
use Framework\Validation\Rule\MinRule;

class ValidationProvider
{
    public function bind(App $app)
    {
        $app->bind('validator', function($app) {
            $manager = new Manager();

            $this->bindRules($app, $manager);
```

© Christopher Pitt 2021
C. Pitt, *Pro PHP 8 MVC*, https://doi.org/10.1007/978-1-4842-6957-2_9

```
            return $manager;
        });
    }

    private function bindRules(App $app, Manager $manager)
    {
        $app->bind('validation.rule.required', fn() => new RequiredRule());
        $app->bind('validation.rule.email', fn() => new EmailRule());
        $app->bind('validation.rule.min', fn() => new MinRule());

        $manager->addRule('required', $app->resolve('validation.rule.
        required'));
        $manager->addRule('email', $app->resolve('validation.rule.email'));
        $manager->addRule('min', $app->resolve('validation.rule.min'));
    }
}
```

This is from `framework/Provider/ValidationProvider.php`.

I am a fan of binding the individual rules to the container (just like we did for the view engines, last chapter) because they can be extended, decorated, and reconfigured.

We could, for instance, resolve the email validation rule and change how it works or override it to provide some new logic. That wouldn't be as straightforward if there was no way to pull it from the container.

Thanks to how we changed the router (to use the container for resolving handlers), I could also remove every route action constructor method. I won't show all of these changes, but they resemble the following:

```
namespace App\Http\Controllers\Products;

use App\Models\Product;
use Framework\Routing\Router;

class ShowProductController
{
    // protected Router $router;

    // public function __construct(Router $router)
```

```
// {
//     $this->router = $router;
// }

public function handle(Router $router)
{
    $parameters = $router->current()->parameters();

    $product = Product::find((int) $parameters['product']);

    return view('products/view', [
        'product' => $product,
        'orderAction' => $router->route('order-product', ['product' =>
        $product->id]),
        'csrf' => csrf(),
    ]);
}
}
```

This is from app/Http/Controllers/Products/ShowProductcontroller.php.

These were the only changes to the codebase. Did you try your hand at moving the validation manager configuration to its own provider? It was a fun experience for me...

Why Should We Test Our Code?

Before we look at the practicalities of testing, it's important to think about why we should be testing. Testing takes many forms, and you're undoubtedly doing a form of testing already.

The most common is keeping a browser or terminal tab open, while you code, and periodically refreshing the browser or running the script related to what you're coding.

This is manual testing, and there's nothing particularly wrong with it. If it's the only testing you're doing, you might be missing out on some important things:

- Are you remembering all the things you *need* to test?

- Are you testing efficiently?

- Do you have up-to-date documentation explaining what needs to be tested to someone else on the team?

249

These things are much harder to achieve without the kind of testing we're going to be exploring in this chapter.

The kind of testing we're about to explore is called automated testing. By design, it solves each of the problems listed in the preceding. Automated testing is what happens when you write code to test your other code that can be run with as little interaction as possible and on the widest range of systems as possible.

Different Types of Tests

There is a lot of information and confusion around the different kinds of tests. We're going to explore a couple, and I'll refer to them as "unit" and "integration."

The main difference between these is that "unit" tests are aimed at a very small section of code and depend on as little else as possible. "Integration" tests, on the other hand, are about testing something like we would if we were doing it by hand. If you're new to testing, then this can be a little confusing.

Where relevant, I'll be sure to describe what kind of tests we're writing and why they are that kind of tests. It's not hugely important to always know or care about the kind of test, but it's helpful to know some of the terminology when talking to other developers about the tests.

Ways We'll Be Testing

We have written a fair bit of code, so there is plenty to test. I'll go over some things I want to test in this chapter and leave the rest for you to test as you feel like. Here are the things I want us to cover:

1. Testing the validation library, to make sure the correct messages are returned and errors are raised at appropriate points

2. Testing the routing library, to make sure routes are dispatched appropriately and with dependencies resolved from the container

3. Testing that the various Whoosh! website pages are working and that registration and login pages are working as expected

This list may seem small, but there's a ton of work to do. As with Chapter 6, we're going to see what popular testing libraries exist and why it's smart to focus our time building tests and helpers for them rather than reinventing a full testing library.

Let's get started!

Putting It All Together

Testing is a vast topic to cover, but most tests happen in three steps:

1. Setting up the conditions as they should be at the beginning of the test

2. Figuring out what the expected outcome is

3. Running the code that you want to generate the expected outcome and comparing the results to the expectations

Every good testing framework makes these things easier to do. We can describe these steps, in code, like this:

```php
// tests use framework classes...
require __DIR__ . '/../vendor/autoload.php';

// validation manager uses $_SESSION...
session_start();

use Framework\Validation\Manager;
use Framework\Validation\Rule\EmailRule;
use Framework\Validation\ValidationException;

class ValidationTest
{
    protected Manager $manager;

    public function setUp()
    {
        $this->manager = new Manager();
        $this->manager->addRule('email', new EmailRule());
    }
```

```php
    public function testInvalidEmailValuesFail()
    {
        $this->setUp();

        $expected = ['email' => ['email should be an email']];

        try {
            $this->manager->validate(['email' => 'foo'], ['email' =>
            ['email']]);
        }
        catch (Throwable $e) {
            assert($e instanceof ValidationException, 'error should be
            thrown');
            assert($e->getErrors()['email'] === $expected['email'],
            'messages should match');
            return;
        }

        throw new Exception('validation did not fail');
    }

    public function testValidEmailValuesPass()
    {
        $this->setUp();

        try {
            $this->manager->validate(['email' => 'foo@bar.com'],
            ['email' => ['email']]);
        }
        catch (Throwable $e) {
            throw new Exception('validation did failed');
            return;
        }
    }
}
```

```
$test = new ValidationTest();
$test->testInvalidEmailValuesFail();
$test->testValidEmailValuesPass();

print 'All tests passed' . PHP_EOL;
```

This is from `tests/ValidationTest.php`.

There's a lot going on here, so let's break it down into smaller parts:

- We have two tests, the first of which ensures the validator will throw a `ValidationException` if an invalid email is passed and the second of which ensures that valid emails won't trigger the email validation exception.

- Both tests expect a validation `Manager`, with the `email` rule added, which we set up in the `setUp` method.

- The first test explicitly declares the expectation, which is that the `ValidationException` will have an email error in it.

- The second test implicitly declares the expectation, which is that no error will occur when a valid email address is validated.

- I call this an acceptably small part of the codebase to test, making this a unit test.

One thing you're going to see is that testing can often take more code than the code it's testing. That's because good tests test more than "the happy path." Good tests also need to test a wide range of failure conditions...

"The happy path" is a phrase that means the path through an interface or piece of code where the interface or code is being used exactly as expected.

A method like `addIntegerToInteger` might expect a couple of integers and return the addition of the two, so "the happy path" is when someone calls it with two integers and expects the numbers to be added together.

Calling it with two strings is not "the happy path," nor is expecting the method to perform multiplication.

There are some things we can leave up to static analysis tools – like that inputs are the correct type. Other things are harder for static analysis to work out, and these are definitely things we should be covering in tests.

As I said, every good testing framework makes these steps easier. They'll do helpful things, like autoloading your framework and application code without you needing to call `require`.

They'll make sure methods like `setUp` are run before each test. They'll run test methods (usually looking for the prefix, like we have added with `testX`) so that we don't need to create new test class instances and manually call the methods.

Some testing frameworks will make it easier to isolate units of code, for testing, or create fake dependencies.

As we learned, with the console commands we added for the database library, some things are not worth the time they would take us to build.

If you'd prefer to create your own testing library from scratch, then go for it! Take a look at what PHPUnit does, and extrapolate from the code we just saw. There's plenty of work for us to do, even if we start off by using PHPUnit, like allowing requests from our tests to pass through the router and then inspecting the response.

Let's install PHPUnit and set up the configuration file it needs to run:

```
composer require --dev phpunit/phpunit
```

PHPUnit's configuration file is an XML file, which defines which test files to run, among other things:

```
<phpunit
    backupGlobals="true"
    bootstrap="vendor/autoload.php"
    colors="true"
>
```

```
<testsuites>
    <testsuite name="Test Suite">
        <directory>tests</directory>
    </testsuite>
</testsuites>
</phpunit>
```

This is from `phpunit.xml`.

This is a stripped-down version of the full configuration: 3. The XML Configuration File – PHPUnit 9.5 Manual. By specifying the `tests` directory, PHPUnit will look for files ending in `Test.php` (by default).

PHPUnit ships with a class that provides some assertion helper methods. We can extend that class and remove some existing boilerplate:

```
// tests use framework classes...
// require __DIR__ . '/../vendor/autoload.php';

// validation manager uses $_SESSION...
session_start();

use Framework\Validation\Manager;
use Framework\Validation\Rule\EmailRule;
use Framework\Validation\ValidationException;

class ValidationTest extends \PHPUnit\Framework\TestCase
{
    protected Manager $manager;

    public function testInvalidEmailValuesFail()
    {
        $manager = new Manager();
        $manager->addRule('email', new EmailRule());

        $expected = ['email' => ['email should be an email']];

        try {
            $manager->validate(['email' => 'foo'], ['email' => ['email']]);
        }
```

```
        catch (Throwable $e) {
            assert($e instanceof ValidationException, 'error should be
            thrown');
            assert($e->getErrors()['email'] === $expected['email'],
            'messages should match');
            return;
        }

        throw new Exception('validation did not fail');
    }

    public function testValidEmailValuesPass()
    {
        $manager = new Manager();
        $manager->addRule('email', new EmailRule());

        try {
            $manager->validate(['email' => 'foo@bar.com'], ['email' =>
            ['email']]);
        }
        catch (Throwable $e) {
            throw new Exception('validation did failed');
            return;
        }
    }
}

// $test = new ValidationTest();
// $test->testInvalidEmailValuesFail();
// $test->testValidEmailValuesPass();

// print 'All tests passed' . PHP_EOL;
```

This is from tests/ValidationTest.php.

The TestCase class automatically calls setUp, and the test runner automatically calls all the methods prefixed with testX.

These test methods are still very cluttered, because we're dealing with exceptions. We only really need the exception in the first method, but maybe we can slim that code down further.

Before that, though, let's run the tests:

vendor/bin/phpunit

PHPUnit isn't showing a test failure, but it's also not showing success. It has methods for saying that an exception is expected when some code runs, but it doesn't have an easy way to look at what that exception contains (in terms of an exception message and nested data).

Let's make a framework helper class that makes inspecting the exception easier to do:

```
namespace Framework\Testing;

use Closure;
use Exception;
use PHPUnit\Framework\TestCase as BaseTestCase;
use Throwable;

class TestCase extends BaseTestCase
{
    protected function assertExceptionThrown(Closure $risky, string
    $exceptionType)
    {
        $result = null;
        $exception = null;

        try {
            $result = $risky();
            $this->fail('exception was not thrown');
        }
        catch (Throwable $e) {
            $actualType = $e::class;

            if ($actualType !== $exceptionType) {
                $this->fail("exception was {$actualType}, but expected
                {$exceptionType}");
            }
```

```
            $exception = $e;
        }

        return [$exception, $result];
    }
}
```

This is from `framework/Testing/TestCase.php`.

This new `assertExceptionThrown` runs a function and records both the exception thrown and the result of the method. If no exception is thrown, the test being run fails.

`$result` is only useful if the expected exception is not being thrown. It's only there to aid in debugging, should the risky closure not produce the desired exception.

This makes the `testValidEmailValuesPass` much cleaner:

```
public function testInvalidEmailValuesFail()
{
    $expected = ['email' => ['email should be an email']];

    // try {

    // }
    // catch (Throwable $e) {
    //      assert($e instanceof ValidationException, 'error should be
    //      thrown');
    //      assert($e->getErrors()['email'] === $expected['email'],
    //      'messages should match');
    //      return;
    // }

    [ $exception ] = $this->assertExceptionThrown(
        fn() => $this->manager->validate(['email' => 'foo'], ['email' =>
        ['email']]),
        ValidationException::class,
    );
```

```
$this->assertEquals($expected, $exception->getErrors());

// throw new Exception('validation did not fail');
}
```

This is from `tests/ValidationTest.php`.

We're also using PHPUnit's `assertEquals` method to compare the full expectation to the full array of errors returned in the exception. Let's add a Composer script to run the tests quicker:

```
"scripts": {
    "serve": "php -S 127.0.0.1:8000 -t public",
    "test": "vendor/bin/phpunit"
},
```

This is from `composer.json`.

Now, we can run the tests with `composer test`. The results look super cool, but just the one test is passing at the moment.

```
.R                                                          2 / 2 (100%)


Time: 00:00.005, Memory: 6.00 MB


There was 1 risky test:


1) ValidationTest::testInvalidEmailValuesFail
This test did not perform any assertions


/Users/assertchris/Source/pro-php-mvc/tests/ValidationTest.php:49


OK, but incomplete, skipped, or risky tests!
Tests: 2, Assertions: 1, Risky: 1.
```

Running the tests with PHPUnit

Let's change the next test to use PHPUnit's assertions. We might as well just check the return value of the `validate` method:

```
public function testValidEmailValuesPass()
{
    // try {
    //     $this->manager->validate(['email' => 'foo@bar.com'], ['email' =>
    //     ['email']]);
    // }
    // catch (Throwable $e) {
    //     throw new Exception('validation did failed');
    //     return;
    // }

    $data = $this->manager->validate(['email' => 'foo@bar.com'], ['email'
    => ['email']]);
    $this->assertEquals($data['email'], 'foo@bar.com');
}
```

This is from `tests/ValidationTest.php`.

It'd be good to add tests for the other two validation rules we already have, but they're going to look very similar to these ones. Maybe you can add them between chapters? (Nudge and wink.)

Testing HTTP Requests

Let's move on to testing that routes load the correct pages, without errors. We could do that by instantiating the router (like the unit tests we just made for validation), but I think it's a good opportunity to make requests to the application.

For setup, we need to start the application up. Then, we can fake HTTP requests to it:

```php
use Framework\App;

class RoutingTest extends Framework\Testing\TestCase
{
    protected App $app;

    public function setUp(): void
    {
        parent::setUp();

        $this->app = App::getInstance();
        $this->app->bind('paths.base', fn() => __DIR__ . '/../');
    }

    public function testHomePageIsShown()
    {
        $_SERVER['REQUEST_METHOD'] = 'GET';
        $_SERVER['REQUEST_URI'] = '/';

        ob_start();
        $this->app->run();
        $html = ob_get_contents();
        ob_end_clean();

        $expected = 'Take a trip on a rocket ship';

        $this->assertStringContainsString($expected, $html);
    }
}
```

This is from tests/RoutingTest.php.

The router uses REQUEST_METHOD and REQUEST_URI to figure out which route to select. We can put our own values in – as though these were values being sent from the browser – and the router will select the home route.

We can fake more intricate requests, like if we wanted to test that the validation error messages were being shown correctly:

```php
public function testRegistrationErrorsAreShown()
{
    $_SERVER['REQUEST_METHOD'] = 'POST';
    $_SERVER['REQUEST_URI'] = '/register';
    $_SERVER['HTTP_REFERER'] = '/register';

    $_POST['email'] = 'foo';
    $_POST['csrf'] = csrf();

    $expected = 'email should be an email';

    $this->assertStringContainsString($expected, $this->app->run());
}
```

This is from `tests/RoutingTest.php`.

Unfortunately, this won't work. In theory, it should, because we're faking the ideal conditions for a form submission to the registration action. The problem is that the application is already sending headers, probably related to starting the session.

```
1) RoutingTest::testRegistrationErrorsAreShown
Cannot modify header information - headers already sent by (output started at /Users/assertchri
s/Source/pro-php-mvc/vendor/phpunit/phpunit/src/Util/Printer.php:104)

/Users/assertchris/Source/pro-php-mvc/framework/helpers.php:35
/Users/assertchris/Source/pro-php-mvc/framework/Routing/Router.php:46
/Users/assertchris/Source/pro-php-mvc/framework/App.php:66
/Users/assertchris/Source/pro-php-mvc/framework/App.php:35
/Users/assertchris/Source/pro-php-mvc/tests/RoutingTest.php:38

ERRORS!
Tests: 4, Assertions: 3, Errors: 1.
Script vendor/bin/phpunit handling the test event returned with error code 2
```

PHP doesn't like it when we try to send headers after any text has already been sent to the browser or terminal. The solution to this problem isn't simple.

We essentially need to start wrapping our responses in response objects that we can inspect to see what they contain without sending their textual content to the browser or terminal.

Let's create this new Response class and bind it to the container:

```php
namespace Framework\Http;

use InvalidArgumentException;

class Response
{
    const REDIRECT = 'REDIRECT';
    const HTML = 'HTML';
    const JSON = 'JSON';

    private string $type = 'HTML';
    private ?string $redirect = null;
    private mixed $content = '';
    private int $status = 200;
    private array $headers = [];

    public function content(mixed $content = null): mixed
    {
        if (is_null($content)) {
            return $this->content;
        }

        $this->content = $content;

        return $this;
    }

    public function status(int $code = null): int|static
    {
```

```php
        if (is_null($code)) {
            return $this->code;
        }

        $this->code = $code;

        return $this;
    }

    public function header(strign $key, string $value): static
    {
        $this->headers[$key] = $value;
        return $this;
    }

    public function redirect(string $redirect = null): mixed
    {
        if (is_null($redirect)) {
            return $this->redirect;
        }

        $this->redirect = $redirect;
        $this->type = static::REDIRECT;
        return $this;
    }

    public function json(mixed $content): static
    {
        $this->content = $content;
        $this->type = static::JSON;
        return $this;
    }

    public function type(string $type = null): string|static
    {
        if (is_null($type)) {
            return $this->type;
        }
```

```php
        $this->type = $type;

        return $this;
    }

    public function send(): string
    {
        foreach ($this->headers as $key => $value) {
            header("{$key}: {$value}");
        }

        if ($this->type === static::HTML) {
            header('Content-Type: text/html');
            http_response_code($this->status);
            print $this->content;
        }

        if ($this->type === static::JSON) {
            header('Content-Type: application/json');
            http_response_code($this->status);
            print json_encode($this->content);
        }

        if ($this->type === static::REDIRECT) {
            header("Location: {$this->redirect}");
            http_response_code($this->code);
        }

        throw new InvalidArgumentException("{$this->type} is not a
        recognised type");
    }
}
```

This is from framework/Http/Response.php.

I think it's a good idea to support the three most common types of responses: HTML, JSON, and redirect responses. Here, we're following a pattern we've followed before, which is to have getters and setters mixed together. It's particularly effective in this case, because we send responses in every controller.

An important difference, between this class and the approach we took before, is that nothing is automatically sent to the browser. We *must* call the send method for that to happen.

Let's bind this class to the container, so that we can use it in the rest of the app:

```
namespace Framework\Provider;

use Framework\App;
use Framework\Http\Response;

class ResponseProvider
{
    public function bind(App $app)
    {
        $app->bind('response', function($app) {
            return new Response();
        });
    }
}
```

This is from `framework/Provider/ResponseProvider.php`.

You're probably thinking; "Hold on. Response isn't a service. Why are we binding it as a service?"

It's not, and this is an odd way to pass it around, but it is something we want to be able to reuse, so that we're adding to an existing response object through the lifecycle of the application.

Now, we can use the response binding to wrap all responses:

```
public function run()
{
    if (session_status() !== PHP_SESSION_ACTIVE) {
        session_start();
    }
```

```
    $basePath = $this->resolve('paths.base');

    $this->configure($basePath);
    $this->bindProviders($basePath);

    return $this->dispatch($basePath);
}
private function dispatch(string $basePath): Response
{
    $router = new Router();

    $this->bind(Router::class, fn() => $router);

    $routes = require "{$basePath}/app/routes.php";
    $routes($router);

    $response = $router->dispatch();

    if (!$response instanceof Response) {
        $response = $this->resolve('response')->content($response);
    }

    return $response;
}
```

This is from `framework/App.php`.

If the controllers return anything other than this response class, we can assume the value should be HTML sent to the browser. Finally, we should change the `public.php` entry point, so that it sends the response:

```
$app = \Framework\App::getInstance();
$app->bind('paths.base', fn() => __DIR__ . '/../');
$app->run()->send();
```

This is from `public/index.php`.

Take a moment to start the server up (which you can do with `composer serve`) and make sure you can still see all the pages.

We can also refactor the redirect helper to use this new method of redirection:

```
if (!function_exists('response')) {
    function response()
    {
        return app('response');
    }
}

if (!function_exists('redirect')) {
    function redirect(string $url)
    {
        return response()->redirect($url);
    }
}
```

This is from `framework/helpers.php`.

The tests also need to be updated to use this new run method:

```
public function testHomePageIsShown()
{
    $_SERVER['REQUEST_METHOD'] = 'GET';
    $_SERVER['REQUEST_URI'] = '/';

    $expected = 'Take a trip on a rocket ship';

    $this->assertStringContainsString($expected, $this->app->run()-
>content());
}

public function testRegistrationErrorsAreShown()
{
    $_SERVER['REQUEST_METHOD'] = 'POST';
    $_SERVER['REQUEST_URI'] = '/register';
    $_SERVER['HTTP_REFERER'] = '/register';
```

```
$_POST['email'] = 'foo';
$_POST['csrf'] = csrf();

$expected = 'email should be an email';

$this->assertStringContainsString($expected, $this->app->run()-
>content());
}
```

This is from `tests/RoutingTest.php`.

With this new abstraction, the error is no longer about headers being sent after content.

```
.F..                                                         4 / 4 (100%)


Time: 00:00.016, Memory: 6.00 MB


There was 1 failure:


1) RoutingTest::testRegistrationErrorsAreShown
Failed asserting that '' contains "email should be an email".


/Users/assertchris/Source/pro-php-mvc/tests/RoutingTest.php:38


FAILURES!
Tests: 4, Assertions: 4, Failures: 1.
Script vendor/bin/phpunit handling the test event returned with error code 1
```

A new error

The problem, now, is that the redirect isn't being sent to the terminal. We need to be a bit smarter about how we inspect responses inside tests. Let's create a response decorator class, which can "follow redirects" in responses, without sending any headers or content to the terminal or browser:

```
namespace Framework\Testing;

use Framework\App;
use Framework\Http\Response;

class TestResponse
{
    private Response $response;

    public function __construct(Response $response)
    {
        $this->response = $response;
    }

    public function isRedirecting(): bool
    {
        return $this->response->type() === Response::REDIRECT;
    }

    public function redirectingTo(): ?string
    {
        return $this->response->redirect();
    }

    public function follow(): static
    {
        while ($this->isRedirecting()) {
            $_SERVER['REQUEST_METHOD'] = 'GET';
            $_SERVER['REQUEST_URI'] = $this->redirectingTo();
            $this->response = App::getInstance()->run();
        }

        return $this;
    }
```

```php
public function __call(string $method, array $parameters = []): mixed
{
    return $this->response->$method(...$parameters);
}
}
```

This is from `framework/Testing/TestResponse.php`.

This also makes our registration errors test a little clearer, in terms of what we're testing:

```php
public function testRegistrationErrorsAreShown()
{
    $_SERVER['REQUEST_METHOD'] = 'POST';
    $_SERVER['REQUEST_URI'] = '/register';
    $_SERVER['HTTP_REFERER'] = '/register';

    $_POST['email'] = 'foo';
    $_POST['csrf'] = csrf();

    $response = new TestResponse($this->app->run());

    $this->assertTrue($response->isRedirecting());
    $this->assertEquals('/register', $response->redirectingTo());

    $response->follow();

    $this->assertStringContainsString('email should be an email',
    $response->content());
}
```

This is from `tests/RoutingTest.php`.

These tests, which almost make full HTTP requests to the application, are examples of integration testing. We're not just testing a class or method: we're testing the full controller functionality, redirects, and errors stored in the session.

It's a less focused kind of testing, but it covers lots of ground in a short space of time. The best test suites have a healthy mixture of unit and integration tests.

And our tests should be passing now!

```
> vendor/bin/phpunit
PHPUnit 9.5.0 by Sebastian Bergmann and contributors.


....                                                          4 / 4 (100%)


Time: 00:00.022, Memory: 6.00 MB

OK (4 tests, 6 assertions)
```

Tests passing

Testing Browser Interaction

The last subject I want to touch on is testing the website as if we're using a browser (but still automating the process). These kinds of tests tend to be brittle, because they depend on the structure of HTML, but they are the only way to test that all your JavaScript code is working...

To achieve this, we're going to pull in another excellent dependency – Symfony Panther. It's a bridge between PHP and the browser:

```
composer require --dev symfony/panther
composer require --dev dbrekelmans/bdi
vendor/bin/bdi detect drivers
```

These commands install Panther and one of the recommended browser drivers. Panther provides a few helpers, for interacting with the browser. It's based on Facebook's WebDriver library. With Panther, we can do all sorts of cool things:

```
use Facebook\WebDriver\WebDriverBy;
use Framework\Testing\TestCase;
use Symfony\Component\Panther\Client;
```

```php
class BrowserTest extends TestCase
{
    public function testLoginForm()
    {
        $client = Client::createFirefoxClient();
        $client->request('GET', 'http://127.0.0.1:8000/register');

        $client->waitFor('.log-in-button');
        $client->executeScript("document.querySelector('.log-in-button').
        click()");

        $client->waitFor('.log-in-errors');
        $element = $client->findElement(WebDriverBy::className('log-in-
        form'));

        $this->assertStringContainsString('password is required', $element-
        >getText());
    }
}
```

This is from `tests/BrowserTest.php`.

If you're using ChromeDriver, instead of GeckoDriver, you should use the `createChromeClient` method instead. These methods start a testing browser, which the code uses to interact with the HTML of the page.

Browser tests are usually a series of steps, in which we wait for stuff to become usable and then use them (by clicking, typing, etc). In this case, we're waiting for a login button, clicking it, and then making sure that the error messages are displayed.

It's not strictly testing JavaScript functionality, but if you need to do that, then this is how you can.

Be sure to add all those helper classes to the HTML of your login form:

```
<form
  method="post"
  action="{{ $logInAction }}"
  class="flex flex-col w-full space-y-4 max-w-xl log-in-form"
>
  @if(isset($_SESSION['login_errors']))
  <ol class="list-disc text-red-500 log-in-errors">
    @foreach($_SESSION['login_errors'] as $field => $errors)
    @foreach($errors as
    $error)
    <li>{{ $error }}</li>
    @endforeach @endforeach
  </ol>
  @endif
  <!-- ... -->
  <button
    type="submit"
    class="bg-indigo-500 rounded-lg p-2 text-white log-in-button"
  >
    Log in
  </button>
</form>
```

This is from `resources/views/users/register.advanced.php`.

If you'd like to see the testing browser work, you can run the tests with a special environment variable:

```
PANTHER_NO_HEADLESS=1 composer test
```

If you're using the correct browser client and you've coded everything up properly, you should see Chromium or Firefox launch and go to the registration page of your website.

You should also see the testing browser click the login button and see the error messages appear as a result.

I recommend looking at the Symfony Panther documentation and the Facebook WebDriver documentation, to learn more about how these libraries work.

Caveats

This has been a whirlwind of a chapter. There's so much to learn about testing and about strutting our application and framework code so that it is easier to test.

There are a bunch of things we could improve in our framework, to make it easier to test. It's not great that we need to start the session in the test file, for example. We're going to be fixing some of these things in the upcoming chapters, but don't let areas for improvement in your framework stop you from trying to test.

There's plenty to do to cement this learning in your mind:

- It would be great to finish testing validation, routing, and form interaction.

- It would be easier to test requests if we had some sort of HTTP request abstraction, just like we have the HTTP response abstraction.

- How could we automate the starting of the website server, at the beginning of the test suite, and stop it after all the tests are run?

How the Pros Do Things

Every good and popular framework has testing helpers, and almost all of them use PHPUnit under the hood. It's a standard for testing in the industry.

That's not to say that you can't or shouldn't try to build your own alternative, but it does mean you can depend on this lovely open source library.

Laravel has many more testing tools, but the underlying approach to testing HTTP responses is the same. Laravel's HTTP classes are built on top of Symfony's HTTP classes.

That means code and approaches that work in Symfony are likely to work in Laravel applications, with very little fuss. It also means an understanding of these classes is essential and transferrable between applications written in both frameworks.

There are many community-supported libraries and approaches to sending different kinds of responses to the browser, like RSS, XML, and streaming responses.

We've already seen Panther, but Laravel has a similar browser testing library, called Dusk. It's not super portable outside of the framework, but if you're browser testing in a Laravel application, then it's a treat to use.

Summary

In this chapter, we learned loads about testing. It's something we should continue doing, as we build more of our framework, but it can be a steep learning curve.

In the next chapter, we're going to start filling out our framework with driver-based libraries to do useful things (like work with sessions and the filesystem).

CHAPTER 10

Config, Cache, Sessions, Filesystems

Now that we've tackled testing and service location, we're in the home stretch of our journey. In this chapter, we're going to make a better way of loading configuration.

We're also going to add drivers for cache, session management, and filesystem access. We'll focus on one to two drivers per area of technology, but we'll build a good base on top of which you can add your own drivers.

What's Changed Since Last Time?

Before we get to the main content of the chapter, I would like to review what I changed between chapters. I set some challenges, toward the end of the previous chapter, and this is a recap of what I did to solve some of those challenges...

I began by cleaning up some of the database configuration we'd moved to the `Model` class. This is what it looked like before I started:

```
public function getConnection(): Connection
{
    if (!isset($this->connection)) {
        $factory = new Factory();

        $factory->addConnector('mysql', function($config) {
            return new MysqlConnection($config);
        });

        $factory->addConnector('sqlite', function($config) {
            return new SqliteConnection($config);
        });
```

© Christopher Pitt 2021
C. Pitt, *Pro PHP 8 MVC*, https://doi.org/10.1007/978-1-4842-6957-2_10

```php
    $config = require basePath() . 'config/database.php';

    $this->connection = $factory->connect($config[$config['default']]);
    }

    return $this->connection;
}
```

This is from `framework/Database/Model.php`.

I thought it would be better to configure this in a provider:

```php
namespace Framework\Provider;

use Framework\App;
use Framework\Database\Factory;
use Framework\Database\Connection\MysqlConnection;
use Framework\Database\Connection\SqliteConnection;

class DatabaseProvider
{
    public function bind(App $app): void
    {
        $app->bind('database', function($app) {
            $factory = new Factory();
            $this->addMysqlConnector($factory);
            $this->addSqliteConnector($factory);

            $config = $this->config($app);

            return $factory->connect($config[$config['default']]);
        });
    }

    private function config(App $app): array
    {
        $base = $app->resolve('paths.base');
        $separator = DIRECTORY_SEPARATOR;
```

```
        return require "{$base}{$separator}config/database.php";
    }

    private function addMysqlConnector($factory): void
    {
        $factory->addConnector('sqlite', function($config) {
            return new SqliteConnection($config);
        });
    }

    private function addSqliteConnector($factory): void
    {
        $factory->addConnector('mysql', function($config) {
            return new MysqlConnection($config);
        });
    }
}
```

This is from `framework/Provider/DatabaseProvider.php`.

This means that anything that needs a preconfigured database connection can access it directly from the container. We can shorten the model code, significantly:

```
public function getConnection(): Connection
{
    if (!isset($this->connection)) {
        $this->connection = app('database');
    }

    return $this->connection;
}
```

This is from `framework/Database/Model.php`.

I spent the rest of the time adding to the automated test suite. I added browser tests for the registration form's validation and unit tests for the remaining validation rules.

I didn't like that I had to keep the server running in one terminal tab while running the browser tests in another, so I figured out a way for the browser tests to "boot" the server as they ran.

To make this work, I had to refactor the `composer serve` command as a framework command:

```php
namespace Framework\Support\Command;

use InvalidArgumentException;
use Symfony\Component\Console\Command\Command;
use Symfony\Component\Console\Input\InputOption;
use Symfony\Component\Console\Input\InputInterface;
use Symfony\Component\Console\Output\OutputInterface;
use Symfony\Component\Process\Process;

class ServeCommand extends Command
{
    protected static $defaultName = 'serve';

    private Process $process;

    protected function configure()
    {
        $this
            ->setDescription('Starts a development server')
            ->setHelp('You can provide an optional host and port, for the
            development server.')
            ->addOption('host', null, InputOption::VALUE_REQUIRED)
            ->addOption('port', null, InputOption::VALUE_REQUIRED);
    }

    protected function execute(InputInterface $input, OutputInterface
    $output): int
    {
        $base = app('paths.base');
        $host = $input->getOption('host') ?: env('APP_HOST', '127.0.0.1');
        $port = $input->getOption('port') ?: env('APP_PORT', '8000');
```

```php
    if (empty($host) || empty($port)) {
        throw new InvalidArgumentException('APP_HOST and APP_PORT both
        need values');
    }

    $this->handleSignals();
    $this->startProcess($host, $port, $base, $output);

    return Command::SUCCESS;
}

private function command(string $host, string $port, string $base):
array
{
    $separator = DIRECTORY_SEPARATOR;

    return [
        PHP_BINARY,
        "-S",
        "{$host}:{$port}",
        "{$base}{$separator}server.php",
    ];
}

private function handleSignals(): void
{
    pcntl_async_signals(true);

    pcntl_signal(SIGTERM, function($signal) {
        if ($signal === SIGTERM) {
            $this->process->signal(SIGKILL);
            exit;
        }
    });
}
```

```php
    private function startProcess(string $host, string $port, string $base,
    OutputInterface $output): void
    {
        $this->process = new Process($this->command($host, $port, $base),
        $base);
        $this->process->setTimeout(PHP_INT_MAX);

        $this->process->start(function($type, $buffer) use ($output) {
            $output->write("<info>{$buffer}</info>");
        });

        $output->writeln("Serving requests at http://{$host}:{$port}");

        $this->process->wait();
    }
}
```

This is from `framework/Support/Command/ServeCommand.php`.

This command encapsulates code to run the PHP development server, but instead of pointing to a public folder, it is pointing to a `server.php` file. This is proxy to `public/index.php`:

```php
$path = __DIR__;
$separator = DIRECTORY_SEPARATOR;
$uri = urldecode(parse_url($_SERVER['REQUEST_URI'], PHP_URL_PATH));

if (is_file("{$path}{$separator}public{$separator}{$uri}")) {
    return false;
}

require_once "{$path}{$separator}public{$separator}index.php";
```

This is from `server.php`.

ServerCommand is also doing some interesting stuff with signals. There's a PHP extension, which installs alongside PHP by default, which you can use to intercept many interrupt signals.

I implemented a signal listener, so that I can gracefully stop the PHP development server when the command is stopped. This is a trick I learned from *Signaling PHP* by Cal Evans.

With this serve command, I could add a PHPUnit extension, which starts the server before the tests and stops it after they've run:

```php
namespace Framework\Testing;

use PHPUnit\Runner\BeforeFirstTestHook;
use PHPUnit\Runner\AfterLastTestHook;
use Symfony\Component\Process\Process;

final class ServerExtension implements BeforeFirstTestHook,
AfterLastTestHook
{
    private Process $process;
    private bool $startedServer = false;

    private function startServer()
    {
        if ($this->serverIsRunning()) {
            $this->startedServer = false;
            return;
        }

        $this->startedServer = true;

        $base = app('paths.base');
        $separator = DIRECTORY_SEPARATOR;

        $this->process = new Process([
            PHP_BINARY,
            "{$base}{$separator}command.php",
            "serve"
        ], $base);
```

```php
    $this->process->start(function($type, $buffer) {
        print $buffer;
    });
}

private function serverIsRunning()
{
    $connection = @fsockopen(
        env('APP_HOST', '127.0.0.1'),
        env('APP_PORT', '8000'),
    );

    if (is_resource($connection)) {
        fclose($connection);
        return true;
    }

    return false;
}

private function stopServer()
{
    if ($this->startedServer) {
        $this->process->signal(SIGTERM);
    }
}

public function executeBeforeFirstTest(): void
{
    $this->startServer();
}

public function executeAfterLastTest(): void
{
    $this->stopServer();
}
}
```

This is from `framework/Testing/ServerExtension.php`.

Here's where we see the SIGTERM signal being sent to the serve command. Without it (and the signal handling), there's a risk that the server isn't shut down when the tests finish running. It's a bit weird, but this is how that happens.

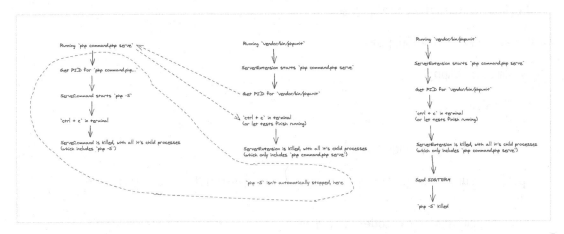

Handling signals

There are other small changes, but these are the important ones to know about. Now, I think we're ready to jump into the content of this chapter!

Better Config Management

We've been using limited configuration data, usually with `require` statements. I think we could do better, by achieving the following goals:

1. Caching configuration as required

2. Abstracting the filesystem details of loading configuration files

There are probably many ways we can store and load configuration (e.g., from a database or third-party service), but we're going to keep it simple. Let's just move the filesystem configuration file access to a central class and bind it to the container.

Laravel uses a kind of dot notation, which I want us to build toward. Configuration lookups take the form config('database.default'), and this leads to the config/database.php file being loaded, everything after the first dot is used to traverse a nested array.

For example, config('database.mysql.username') is loading ['mysql']['username'] from config/database.php. This isn't too much work to replicate...

Let's begin with the Config class:

```
namespace Framework\Support;

use Framework\App;

class Config
{
    private array $loaded = [];

    public function get(string $key, mixed $default = null): mixed
    {
        $segments = explode('.', $key);
        $file = array_shift($segments);

        if (!isset($this->loaded[$file])) {
            $base = App::getInstance()->resolve('paths.base');
            $separator = DIRECTORY_SEPARATOR;

            $this->loaded[$file] = (array) require "{$base}{$separator}
            config{$separator}{$file}.php";
        }

        if ($value = $this->withDots($this->loaded[$file], $segments)) {
            return $value;
        }

        return $default;
    }

    private function withDots(array $array, array $segments): mixed
    {
        $current = $array;
```

```
    foreach ($segments as $segment) {
        if (!isset($current[$segment])) {
            return null;
        }

        $current = $current[$segment];
    }

    return $current;
    }
}
```

This is from `framework/Support/Config.php`.

We begin by deconstructing the $key to the configuration value we want. The first segment is the file name, and the rest are used for the nested lookup.

The `withDots` is an iterative approach to traversing the nested array, but a recursive approach would work just as well.

This needs to be bound to the container, so that it's easier to use:

```
namespace Framework\Provider;

use Framework\App;
use Framework\Support\Config;

class ConfigProvider
{
    public function bind(App $app): void
    {
        $app->bind('config', function($app) {
            return new Config();
        });
    }
}
```

This is from `framework/Provider/ConfigProvider.php`.

Add the ConfigProvider class to `config/providers.php`, so that it is loaded with the application. It should be the first entry, so that subsequent providers have access to the new config abstraction...

We can now clean up various bits of the framework that use configuration. Here's how the database provider code can be cleaned up:

```php
public function bind(App $app): void
{
    $app->bind('database', function($app) {
        $factory = new Factory();
        $this->addMysqlConnector($factory);
        $this->addSqliteConnector($factory);

        // $config = $this->config($app);
        $config = $app->resolve('config')->get('database');

        return $factory->connect($config[$config['default']]);
    });
}

// private function config(App $app): array
// {
//     $base = $app->resolve('paths.base');
//     $separator = DIRECTORY_SEPARATOR;

//     return require "{$base}{$separator}config/database.php";
// }
```

This is from `framework/Provider/DatabaseProvider.php`.

We can make this even better, by creating a config helper:

```php
if (!function_exists('config')) {
    function config(string $key, mixed $default = null): mixed
    {
        return app('config')->get($key, $default);
    }
}
```

This is from `framework/helpers.php`.

The final database provider code looks like this:

```php
public function bind(App $app): void
{
    $app->bind('database', function($app) {
        $factory = new Factory();
        $this->addMysqlConnector($factory);
        $this->addSqliteConnector($factory);

        $config = config('database');

        return $factory->connect($config[$config['default']]);
    });
}
```

This is from `framework/Provider/DatabaseProvider.php`.

Aside from making it easier to use configuration, this abstraction also makes configuration management more efficient – because configuration files are only loaded once.

Now that we have this, we can use more and more configuration files (for cache, sessions, and filesystems) with little effort!

Cache

I can think of many different cache providers, but most of them involve third-party services or servers that run alongside the web server. Let's implement support for the following kinds of simpler cache providers:

1. In-memory cache (i.e., the same kind we're using to cache the config)

2. Filesystem cache

3. Memcache

Memcache is a server that runs alongside the web server, which means we need to install it for this cache driver to function. If you are having trouble installing this, then you could skip this particular "driver"…

We need a similar factory setup to what we're doing for database connections:

```
namespace Framework\Cache;

use Closure;
use Framework\Cache\Driver\Driver;
use Framework\Cache\Exception\DriverException;

class Factory
{
    protected array $drivers;

    public function addDriver(string $alias, Closure $driver): static
    {
        $this->drivers[$alias] = $driver;
        return $this;
    }

    public function connect(array $config): Driver
    {
        if (!isset($config['type'])) {
            throw new DriverException('type is not defined');
        }
```

```
    $type = $config['type'];

    if (isset($this->drivers[$type])) {
        return $this->drivers[$type]($config);
    }

    throw new DriverException('unrecognised type');
    }
}
```

This is from `framework/Cache/Factory.php`.

DriverException is an empty subclass of RuntimeException. This is what the cache config file looks like:

```
return [
    'default' => 'memory',
    'memory' => [
        'type' => 'memory',
        'seconds' => 31536000,
    ],
];
```

This is from `config/cache.php`.

It's really simple, at the moment, but will get more complex as we add additional drivers. 31536000 seconds is 1 year, which we'll use as the default cache expiry value. The Driver interface is a little more interesting, though:

```
namespace Framework\Cache\Driver;

interface Driver
{
    /**
     * Tell if a value is cached (still)
     */
    public function has(string $key): bool;
```

```php
/**
 * Get a cached value
 */
public function get(string $key, mixed $default = null): mixed;

/**
 * Put a value into the cache, for an optional number of seconds
 */
public function put(string $key, mixed $value, int $seconds = null):
static;

/**
 * Remove a single cached value
 */
public function forget(string $key): static;

/**
 * Remove all cached values
 */
public function flush(): static;
}
```

This is from `framework/Cache/Driver/Driver.php`.

We can create an in-memory driver, by connecting each of these method signatures to an internal array:

```php
namespace Framework\Cache\Driver;

class MemoryDriver implements Driver
{
    private array $config = [];
    private array $cached = [];

    public function __construct(array $config)
    {
        $this->config = $config;
    }
```

```php
public function has(string $key): bool
{
    return isset($this->cached[$key]) && $this->cached[$key]['expires']
    > time();
}

public function get(string $key, mixed $default = null): mixed
{
    if ($this->has($key)) {
        return $this->cached[$key]['value'];
    }

    return $default;
}

public function put(string $key, mixed $value, int $seconds = null):
static
{
    if (!is_int($seconds)) {
        $seconds = (int) $this->config['seconds'];
    }

    $this->cached[$key] = [
        'value' => $value,
        'expires' => time() + $seconds,
    ];

    return $this;
}

public function forget(string $key): static
{
    unset($this->cached[$key]);
    return $this;
}
```

```php
    public function flush(): static
    {
        $this->cached = [];
        return $this;
    }
}
```

This is from framework/Cache/Driver/MemoryDriver.php.

The has and get methods look similar to what we did with the Config class, with the addition of an expires key. When someone tells us how many seconds to cache a value for, we add those seconds to the unix timestamp. We can compare that to a unix timestamp (in the future) to work out if the value should expire.

Let's wire this up, in a provider, so we can get to it quickly:

```php
namespace Framework\Provider;

use Framework\App;
use Framework\Cache\Factory;
use Framework\Cache\Driver\MemoryDriver;

class CacheProvider
{
    public function bind(App $app): void
    {
        $app->bind('cache', function($app) {
            $factory = new Factory();
            $this->addMemoryDriver($factory);

            $config = config('cache');

            return $factory->connect($config[$config['default']]);
        });
    }
```

```
    private function addMemoryDriver($factory): void
    {
        $factory->addDriver('memory', function($config) {
            return new MemoryDriver($config);
        });
    }
}
```

This is from `framework/Provider/CacheProvider.php`.

We can make use of this to store bits of data that aren't likely to change very often:

```
$cache = app('cache');
$products = Product::all();

$productsWithRoutes = array_map(function ($product) use ($router) {
    $key = "route-for-product-{$product->id}";

    if (!$cache->has($key)) {
        $cache->put($key, $router->route('view-product', ['product' =>
        $product->id]));
    }

    $product->route = $cache->get($key);

    return $product;
}, $products);

return view('home', [
    'products' => $productsWithRoutes,
]);
```

This is from `app/Http/Controllers/ShowHomePageController.php`.

In this example, we can work out the route for each product, once, and store it in cache.

Don't forget to add the `CacheProvider` class to `config/providers.php`, so that it is loaded with the application.

The memory driver is a little useless while using the PHP development server, because the memory is cleared after each page is returned to the browser. It's useful for testing purposes or in an environment where the memory isn't cleared after every request.

Let's add the next driver, where cached values are stored in the filesystem:

```php
namespace Framework\Cache\Driver;

use Framework\App;

class FileDriver implements Driver
{
    private array $config = [];
    private array $cached = [];

    public function __construct(array $config)
    {
        $this->config = $config;
    }

    public function has(string $key): bool
    {
        $data = $this->cached[$key] = $this->read($key);

        return isset($data['expires']) and $data['expires'] > time();
    }

    private function path(string $key): string
    {
        $base = $this->base();
        $separator = DIRECTORY_SEPARATOR;
        $key = sha1($key);

        return "{$base}{$separator}{$key}.json";
    }
}
```

```php
private function base(): string
{
    $base = App::getInstance()->resolve('paths.base');
    $separator = DIRECTORY_SEPARATOR;

    return "{$base}{$separator}storage{$separator}framework{$separator}
    cache";
}

private function read(string $key)
{
    $path = $this->path($key);

    if (!is_file($path)) {
        return [];
    }

    return json_decode(file_get_contents($path), true);
}

public function get(string $key, mixed $default = null): mixed
{
    if ($this->has($key)) {
        return $this->cached[$key]['value'];
    }

    return $default;
}

public function put(string $key, mixed $value, int $seconds = null):
static
{
    if (!is_int($seconds)) {
        $seconds = (int) $this->config['seconds'];
    }
```

```php
    $data = $this->cached[$key] = [
        'value' => $value,
        'expires' => time() + $seconds,
    ];

    return $this->write($key, $data);
}

private function write(string $key, mixed $value): static
{
    file_put_contents($this->path($key), json_encode($value));
    return $this;
}

public function forget(string $key): static
{
    unset($this->cached[$key]);

    $path = $this->path($key);

    if (is_file($path)) {
        unlink($path);
    }

    return $this;
}

public function flush(): static
{
    $this->cached = [];

    $base = $this->base();
    $separator = DIRECTORY_SEPARATOR;

    $files = glob("{$base}{$separator}*.json");

    foreach ($files as $file){
        if (is_file($file)) {
            unlink($file);
        }
    }
```

```
        return $this;
    }
}
```

This is from `framework/Cache/Driver/FileDriver.php`.

Here, we keep the idea of an internal cache array, but only so that we can cut down on reading the same file multiple times. Cache values are saved to JSON files, along with their expiry time.

This is not an efficient cache driver, so it's only really useful for situations where no better alternative driver is available or where the only cached values take significantly longer to generate than multiple filesystem reads and writes.

Let's extend the config for this filesystem driver, as well as the Memcache driver we're about to add:

```
return [
    'default' => 'memcache',
    'memory' => [
        'type' => 'memory',
        'seconds' => 31536000,
    ],
    'file' => [
        'type' => 'file',
        'seconds' => 31536000,
    ],
    'memcache' => [
        'type' => 'memcache',
        'host' => '127.0.0.1',
        'port' => 11211,
        'seconds' => 31536000,
    ],
];
```

This is from config/cache.php.

The final cache driver uses Memcache:

```php
namespace Framework\Cache\Driver;

use Memcached;

class MemcacheDriver implements Driver
{
    private array $config = [];
    private Memcached $memcache;

    public function __construct(array $config)
    {
        $this->config = $config;

        $this->memcache = new Memcached();
        $this->memcache->addServer($config['host'], $config['port']);
    }

    public function has(string $key): bool
    {
        return $this->memcache->get($key) !== false;
    }

    public function get(string $key, mixed $default = null): mixed
    {
        if ($value = $this->memcache->get($key)) {
            return $value;
        }

        return $default;
    }
```

```php
public function put(string $key, mixed $value, int $seconds = null):
static
{
    if (!is_int($seconds)) {
        $seconds = (int) $this->config['seconds'];
    }

    $this->memcache->set($key, $value, time() + $seconds);
    return $this;
}

public function forget(string $key): static
{
    $this->memcache->delete($key);
    return $this;
}

public function flush(): static
{
    $this->memcache->flush();
    return $this;
}
}
```

This is from framework/Cache/MemcacheDriver.php.

This is significantly quicker to implement than the filesystem driver, because Memcache does a lot of the filesystem and serialization operations behind the scenes.

The only tricky bit is that the Memcache instance is created in the constructor, which would probably be better to do via getters and setters or constructor injection (wink).

Let's add both of these new drivers to the provider:

```php
public function bind(App $app): void
{
    $app->bind('cache', function($app) {
        $factory = new Factory();
        $this->addFileDriver($factory);
```

```
        $this->addMemcacheDriver($factory);
        $this->addMemoryDriver($factory);

        $config = config('cache');

        return $factory->connect($config[$config['default']]);
    });
}

private function addFileDriver($factory): void
{
    $factory->addDriver('file', function($config) {
        return new FileDriver($config);
    });
}

private function addMemcacheDriver($factory): void
{
    $factory->addDriver('memcache', function($config) {
        return new MemcacheDriver($config);
    });
}

private function addMemoryDriver($factory): void
{
    $factory->addDriver('memory', function($config) {
        return new MemoryDriver($config);
    });
}
```

This is from `framework/Provider/CacheProvider.php`.

Spend a few minutes switching the default cache provider, from memory to file to memcache. I find it interesting how well the system works while using very different tech (under the hood), at the change of a single config variable.

Sessions

We've already been using sessions, but let's formalize that code inside a similar factor/ driver arrangement. We'll continue to support the native session management – with better initialization and neat get and put methods.

While it's possible to make and use other session drivers, the exercise gets a bit tedious given what we've already seen in this chapter. If you feel challenged to do so, I recommend trying to add additional session drivers between chapters.

Let's create another factory and corresponding driver interface:

```
namespace Framework\Session;

use Closure;
use Framework\Session\Driver\Driver;
use Framework\Session\Exception\DriverException;

class Factory
{
    protected array $drivers;

    public function addDriver(string $alias, Closure $driver): static
    {
        $this->drivers[$alias] = $driver;
        return $this;
    }

    public function connect(array $config): Driver
    {
        if (!isset($config['type'])) {
            throw new DriverException('type is not defined');
        }

        $type = $config['type'];

        if (isset($this->drivers[$type])) {
            return $this->drivers[$type]($config);
        }
```

```
        throw new DriverException('unrecognised type');
    }
}
```

This is from framework/Session/Factory.php.

This is exactly the same as the cache factory class. Come to think of it. Perhaps this is a good candidate for abstraction – a generic Factory class that these libraries can reuse...

The interface is different form the one we used in the cache library:

```
namespace Framework\Session\Driver;

interface Driver
{
    /**
     * Tell if a value is session
     */
    public function has(string $key): bool;

    /**
     * Get a session value
     */
    public function get(string $key, mixed $default = null): mixed;

    /**
     * Put a value into the session
     */
    public function put(string $key, mixed $value): static;

    /**
     * Remove a single session value
     */
    public function forget(string $key): static;
```

```
/**
 * Remove all session values
 */
public function flush(): static;
}
```

This is from `framework/Session/Driver/Driver.php`.

The main difference is that session methods don't care about expiry times. If expiry is managed, anywhere, it should be part of config and set when the session is started.

The native session driver looks like this:

```
namespace Framework\Session\Driver;

class NativeDriver implements Driver
{
    private array $config = [];

    public function __construct(array $config)
    {
        $this->config = $config;

        if (session_status() !== PHP_SESSION_ACTIVE) {
            session_start();
        }
    }

    public function has(string $key): bool
    {
        $prefix = $this->config['prefix'];
        return isset($_SESSION["{$prefix}{$key}"]);
    }

    public function get(string $key, mixed $default = null): mixed
    {
        $prefix = $this->config['prefix'];
```

```php
        if (isset($_SESSION["{$prefix}{$key}"])) {
            return $_SESSION["{$prefix}{$key}"];
        }

        return $default;
    }

    public function put(string $key, mixed $value): static
    {
        $prefix = $this->config['prefix'];
        $_SESSION["{$prefix}{$key}"] = $value;
        return $this;
    }

    public function forget(string $key): static
    {
        $prefix = $this->config['prefix'];
        unset($_SESSION["{$prefix}{$key}"]);
        return $this;
    }

    public function flush(): static
    {
        foreach (array_keys($_SESSION) as $key) {
            if (str_starts_with($key, $prefix)) {
                unset($_SESSION[$key]);
            }
        }

        return $this;
    }
}
```

This is from framework/Session/Driver/NativeDriver.php.

One thing to point out is that we're storing session variables with keys that are prefixed with a configurable prefix. We do this so that the framework can coexist with other libraries that might also store values in the session, without the likelihood of key collisions.

Since we're moving the call to session_start to this class, we can remove it from the App class:

```php
public function run()
{
    // if (session_status() !== PHP_SESSION_ACTIVE) {
    //     session_start();
    // }

    $basePath = $this->resolve('paths.base');

    $this->configure($basePath);
    $this->bindProviders($basePath);

    return $this->dispatch($basePath);
}
```

This is from framework/App.php.

Now, we need the session config file and the provider that will bind it to the container:

```php
return [
    'default' => 'native',
    'native' => [
        'type' => 'native',
        'prefix' => 'framework_',
    ],
];
```

This is from config/session.php.

```
namespace Framework\Provider;

use Framework\App;
use Framework\Session\Factory;
use Framework\Session\Driver\NativeDriver;

class SessionProvider
{
    public function bind(App $app): void
    {
        $app->bind('session', function($app) {
            $factory = new Factory();
            $this->addNativeDriver($factory);

            $config = config('session');

            return $factory->connect($config[$config['default']]);
        });
    }

    private function addNativeDriver($factory): void
    {
        $factory->addDriver('native', function($config) {
            return new NativeDriver($config);
        });
    }
}
```

This is from `framework/Provider/SessionProvider.php`.

This looks like another candidate for abstraction, since it's basically the same as the CacheProvider class...

Don't forget to add the `SessionProvider` class to `config/providers.php`, so that it is loaded with the application.

This means we can now use the session from anywhere and without needing to bootstrap it every time:

```
app('session')->put(
    'hits', app('session')->get('hits', 0) + 1
);
```

Filesystems

The last library we'll look at, in this chapter, is for filesystems. There are a number of things we could use filesystems for:

1. Loading template-related files

2. Loading internationalization files, to display locale-specific UI labels

3. Storing application assets like images, videos, and audio files

There are also a variety of places we could store things – a variety of systems that qualify as filesystems:

1. The local server filesystem

2. Cloud-based object stores, like S3 and GFS

3. Infrastructural services, like FTP and SFTP

We can go about building a few of these drivers, but I thought this would be a good opportunity to see what would be involved in "wrapping" an existing filesystem library in our own API.

We're going to use a library called Flysystem, but we're going to present it through our own lens.

Let's install it using

```
composer require league/flysystem
```

Now, let's create another factory, using all of the drivers Flysystem natively ships:

```php
namespace Framework\Filesystem;

use Closure;
use Framework\Filesystem\Driver\Driver;
use Framework\Filesystem\Exception\DriverException;

class Factory
{
    protected array $drivers;

    public function addDriver(string $alias, Closure $driver): static
    {
        $this->drivers[$alias] = $driver;
        return $this;
    }

    public function connect(array $config): Driver
    {
        if (!isset($config['type'])) {
            throw new DriverException('type is not defined');
        }

        $type = $config['type'];

        if (isset($this->drivers[$type])) {
            return $this->drivers[$type]($config);
        }

        throw new DriverException('unrecognised type');
    }
}
```

This is from framework/Filesystem/Factory.php.

More of the same...

Let's create a config file for the filesystem drivers:

```
return [
    'default' => 'local',
    'local' => [
        'type' => 'local',
        'path' => __DIR__ . '/../storage/app',
    ],
    's3' => [
        'type' => 's3',
        'key' => '',
        'secret' => '',
        'token' => '',
        'region' => '',
        'bucket' => '',
    ],
    'ftp' => [
        'type' => 'ftp',
        'host' => '',
        'root' => '',
        'username' => '',
        'password' => '',
    ],
];
```

This is from `config/filesystem.php`.

Instead of an interface, we can use an abstract class to define the drivers' signatures. That's because we're not actually implementing any of their functionality – we're just instantiating the Flysystem drivers:

```php
namespace Framework\Filesystem\Driver;

use League\Flysystem\Filesystem;

abstract class Driver
{
    protected Filesystem $filesystem;

    public function __construct(array $config)
    {
        $this->filesystem = $this->connect($config);
    }

    abstract protected function connect(array $config): Filesystem;

    public function list(string $path, bool $recursive = false): iterable
    {
        return $this->filesystem->listContents($path, $recursive);
    }

    public function exists(string $path): bool
    {
        return $this->filesystem->fileExists($path);
    }

    public function get(string $path): string
    {
        return $this->filesystem->read($path);
    }

    public function put(string $path, mixed $value): static
    {
        $this->filesystem->write($path, $value);
        return $this;
    }

    public function delete(string $path): static
    {
        $this->filesystem->delete($path);
```

```
        return $this;
    }
}
```

This is from `framework/Filesystem/Driver/Driver.php`.

I built these methods by studying the Flysystem documentation. Each Flysystem method is "wrapped" in a method that matches the pattern we've created with the other libraries.

The only method that each driver needs to implement is the abstract `connect` method. This is what that looks like, in the `LocalDriver` class:

```
namespace Framework\Filesystem\Driver;

use League\Flysystem\Filesystem;
use League\Flysystem\Local\LocalFilesystemAdapter;

class LocalDriver extends Driver
{
    protected function connect()
    {
        $adapter = new LocalFilesystemAdapter($this->config['path']);
        $this->filesystem = new Filesystem($adapter);
    }
}
```

This is from `framework/Filesystem/Driver/LocalDriver.php`.

Remember, we also need a provider that binds these classes in the container:

```
namespace Framework\Provider;

use Framework\App;
use Framework\Filesystem\Factory;
use Framework\Filesystem\Driver\LocalDriver;
```

```php
class FilesystemProvider
{
    public function bind(App $app): void
    {
        $app->bind('filesystem', function($app) {
            $factory = new Factory();
            $this->addLocalDriver($factory);

            $config = config('filesystem');

            return $factory->connect($config[$config['default']]);
        });
    }

    private function addLocalDriver($factory): void
    {
        $factory->addDriver('local', function($config) {
            return new LocalDriver($config);
        });
    }
}
```

This is from `framework/Provider/FilesystemProvider.php`.

Finally, this provider needs to be added to `config/providers.php`. This file has grown over the course of this chapter, so here's what the final provider config file looks like:

```php
return [
    // load config first, so the rest can use it...
    \Framework\Provider\ConfigProvider::class,

    \Framework\Provider\CacheProvider::class,
    \Framework\Provider\DatabaseProvider::class,
    \Framework\Provider\FilesystemProvider::class,
    \Framework\Provider\ResponseProvider::class,
    \Framework\Provider\SessionProvider::class,
```

```
    \Framework\Provider\ValidationProvider::class,
    \Framework\Provider\ViewProvider::class,
];
```

This is from `config/providers.php`.

The filesystem abstraction can now be accessed from anywhere in the application, as in this example:

```
if (!app('filesystem')->exists('hits.txt')) {
    app('filesystem')->put('hits.txt', '');
}

app('filesystem')->put(
    'hits.txt',
    (int) app('filesystem')->get('hits.txt', 0) + 1,
);
```

Caveats

We've created the cache, session, and filesystem libraries in record time. There are a few things left to do that would make these much better:

- We only created one session driver. It would be cool if we had more drivers, here, but it would most certainly involve using the built-in session driver methods to do well...

- We only "wrapped" one of the Flysystem adapters – in the local driver. Using the config we set up and the pattern we used, do you think you could add S3 and FTP support?

- Toward the end, it became clear that some of these classes can be reused – particularly the Factory and Provider classes. Not all factories will be the same (e.g., the database factory), and not all providers will be the same (e.g., the validation provider). For the factories and providers that are very similar, this could reduce the amount of code we need to maintain...

- All of our config is untyped and unchecked. We're making many assumptions about the structure and presence of config values, so it would be useful to add some safety here.

- It would be great to reuse some of these libraries inside other ones, like reusing the filesystem library to support file-based session storage. Are you up to the challenge?

Summary

In this chapter, we created a useful configuration abstraction and then used it to implement a number of key framework components. Most popular frameworks include these components and then some.

In the following chapter, we're going to implement a few more, as we round out our time together. Try completing some of the challenges before the next chapter, so that your knowledge of these components grows.

CHAPTER 11

Queues, Logging, Emails

We're in the final code chapter, and we've come a long way to get here. Continuing in the theme of the last chapter, we're going to round out our journey by creating another three libraries: this time for queuing slow operations, logging errors, and sending emails.

We're going to look at some great lower-level libraries to repackage, as we create the developer experience that makes our framework desirable among developers of all skill sets.

In the Meantime...

I'd like to go over some things that I worked on between chapters, cleaning up bits of the framework and application code. There are a handful of smaller changes, but two stand out as significant changes:

1. Creating a better exception handling system

2. Refactoring about half the providers that only provide driver-based factories

Better Exception Handling

In the beginning of our journey, we created the router. Part of that was dealing with exceptions that are thrown as routes are dispatched. Later, we added to the potential list of exceptions, by intercepting and reacting to validation exceptions.

This is what the code looked like, until I started messing with it:

```php
public function dispatch()
{
    $paths = $this->paths();

    $requestMethod = $_SERVER['REQUEST_METHOD'] ?? 'GET';
```

317

© Christopher Pitt 2021
C. Pitt, *Pro PHP 8 MVC*, https://doi.org/10.1007/978-1-4842-6957-2_11

```php
    $requestPath = $_SERVER['REQUEST_URI'] ?? '/';

    $matching = $this->match($requestMethod, $requestPath);

    if ($matching) {
        $this->current = $matching;

        try {
            return $matching->dispatch();
        }
        catch (Throwable $e) {
            if ($e instanceof ValidationException) {
                $_SESSION[$e->getSessionName()] = $e->getErrors();
                return redirect($_SERVER['HTTP_REFERER']);
            }

            if (isset($_ENV['APP_ENV']) && $_ENV['APP_ENV'] === 'dev') {
                $whoops = new Run();
                $whoops->pushHandler(new PrettyPageHandler);
                $whoops->register();
                throw $e;
            }

            return $this->dispatchError();
        }
    }

    if (in_array($requestPath, $paths)) {
        return $this->dispatchNotAllowed();
    }

    return $this->dispatchNotFound();
}
```

This is from framework/Routing/Router.php.

There's a bunch of stuff that doesn't really belong here. The router shouldn't know about sessions or the validation library. If either of those things is disabled (e.g., to speed up response times), then routing breaks.

The router also shouldn't care about how we present helpful error messages in development.

We put these things here because we had no better place to put them and because they are triggered as part of the routing process. We needed a better solution...

I addressed this problem by creating a new support class, called ExceptionHandler:

```php
namespace Framework\Support;

use Framework\Validation\Exception\ValidationException;
use Throwable;
use Whoops\Handler\PrettyPageHandler;
use Whoops\Run;

class ExceptionHandler
{
    public function showThrowable(Throwable $throwable)
    {
        if ($throwable instanceof ValidationException) {
            return $this->showValidationException($throwable);
        }

        if (isset($_ENV['APP_ENV']) && $_ENV['APP_ENV'] === 'dev') {
            $this->showFriendlyThrowable($throwable);
        }
    }

    public function showValidationException(ValidationException $exception)
    {
        if ($session = session()) {
            $session->put($exception->getSessionName(), $exception-
            >getErrors());
        }

        return redirect(env('HTTP_REFERER'));
    }
```

```
    public function showFriendlyThrowable(Throwable $throwable)
    {
        $whoops = new Run();
        $whoops->pushHandler(new PrettyPageHandler());
        $whoops->register();

        throw $throwable;
    }
}
```

This is from `framework/Support/ExceptionHandler.php`.

This new class has the responsibility of deciding what to do with various exceptions that the framework can throw. We haven't used this control flow strategy much, but at least now we have a better way of using it.

It's broken up into two main parts:

1. Figuring out what the type of Throwable is

2. Doing something with it – whether that means redirecting or displaying a helpful error page in development

It's already a better solution than putting this code in the router, but it could be better by allowing developers to add their own exception handling into the mix. The idea is one I've seen in Laravel, and there they provide a template for this handling in all new applications.

New applications come with a subclass of this handle in their application folder. I've replicated this behavior with a new application class:

```
namespace App\Exceptions;

use Framework\Support\ExceptionHandler;
use Throwable;

class Handler extends ExceptionHandler
{
    public function showThrowable(Throwable $throwable)
    {
        // add in some reporting...
```

```
    return parent::showThrowable($throwable);
    }
}
```

This is from app/Exceptions/Handler.php.

This has a couple benefits:

1. Developers can add their own exception control flow: they can throw exceptions in routes (for exceptional circumstances) and figure out what to do with any of those in a central place.

2. It's not possible to add custom error logging and handling for exceptional circumstances originating from the framework internals.

In order for the framework to know which handler to send these exceptions to, we need some system of identifying the appropriate class. I figured a config file would work:

```
return [
    'exceptions' => \App\Exceptions\Handler::class,
];
```

This is from config/handlers.php.

And then we need to use this config file to send the exceptions:

```
public function dispatch()
{
    $paths = $this->paths();

    $requestMethod = $_SERVER['REQUEST_METHOD'] ?? 'GET';
    $requestPath = $_SERVER['REQUEST_URI'] ?? '/';

    $matching = $this->match($requestMethod, $requestPath);
```

```php
    if ($matching) {
        $this->current = $matching;

        try {
            return $matching->dispatch();
        }
        catch (Throwable $e) {
            $result = null;

            if ($handler = config('handlers.exceptions')) {
                $instance = new $handler();

                if ($result = $instance->showThrowable($e)) {
                    return $result;
                }
            }

            return $this->dispatchError();
        }
    }

    if (in_array($requestPath, $paths)) {
        return $this->dispatchNotAllowed();
    }

    return $this->dispatchNotFound();
}
```

This is from `framework/Routing/Router.php`.

Using this pattern, we've successfully removed most of the exception handling specifics from the router. It still needs to know where to send the exceptions, but we could further remove this detail by creating an `App::handleException` method, which does this same handler forwarding.

I stopped short of this last step, because I think it becomes less about the objective separation of responsibilities and more about personal preference.

Refactoring Providers

In the previous chapter, I mentioned how many of the providers and factories use similar code to achieve the same results – in particular, the providers that

1. Created a factor instance

2. Added a number of drivers to the factor

3. Resolved config for the library

Are all using the exact same code? After careful review, I realized that we still needed all the factory class (because of type hinting) but that the providers could inherit from a single base:

```php
namespace Framework\Support;

use Framework\App;

abstract class DriverProvider
{
    final public function bind(App $app): void
    {
        $name = $this->name();
        $factory = $this->factory();
        $drivers = $this->drivers();

        $app->bind($name, function ($app) use ($name, $factory, $drivers) {
            foreach ($drivers as $key => $value) {
                $factory->addDriver($key, $value);
            }

            $config = config($name);

            return $factory->connect($config[$config['default']]);
        });
    }

    abstract protected function name(): string;
    abstract protected function factory(): mixed;
    abstract protected function drivers(): array;
}
```

This is from `framework/Support/DriverProvider.php`.

Now, instead of repeating this pattern, subclasses of this provider can focus on providing a compatible factory and list of drivers to add to it. The factory interface looks like this:

```
namespace Framework\Support;

use Closure;

interface DriverFactory
{
    public function addDriver(string $alias, Closure $driver): static;
    public function connect(array $config): mixed;
}
```

This is from `framework/Support/DriverFactory.php`.

This means the providers can slim down, and all tend to look like this:

```
namespace Framework\Provider;

use Framework\Cache\Factory;
use Framework\Cache\Driver\FileDriver;
use Framework\Cache\Driver\MemcacheDriver;
use Framework\Cache\Driver\MemoryDriver;
use Framework\Support\DriverProvider;
use Framework\Support\DriverFactory;

class CacheProvider extends DriverProvider
{
    protected function name(): string
    {
        return 'cache';
    }
```

```php
protected function factory(): DriverFactory
{
    return new Factory();
}

protected function drivers(): array
{
    return [
        'file' => function($config) {
            return new FileDriver($config);
        },
        'memcache' => function($config) {
            return new MemcacheDriver($config);
        },
        'memory' => function($config) {
            return new MemoryDriver($config);
        },
    ];
}
}
```

This is from `framework/Provider/CacheProvider.php`.

That feels much better! And I'm sure we can reuse the pattern for the libraries we make in this chapter.

Queuing

Queuing is about taking slow operations outside of the request/response cycle. If someone's interacting with your website and asks for something that will take time to do (like send an email or generate a report), you could let them wait for the processing to complete, or you could do it in the background and notify them when it is complete.

How that notification happens is a different matter altogether, but one way is to send them an email. We'll show an example of this by the end of the chapter.

This queuing can happen in a number of ways, from storing work orders in a text file to putting them into a cache to using services specifically designed to make storage and retrieval of messages easier.

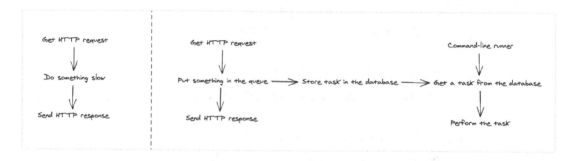

Queueing tasks

Let's build a database-based queueing system, with the following main components:

1. A database table and provider/factory library for putting stuff into the database table

2. A terminal command for pulling tasks out of the database and running them

This is the simplest interface I can think of:

```
app('queue')->push(function($user) {
    // send a mail to the user...
}, $user);
```

push is an interesting name for this method, because it describes the process of putting a task onto the queue. It's similar to PHP's array_push method, and we'll build a corresponding shift method.

To facilitate this functionality, we need a migration that stores serialized parameters (like $user) and also serialized closures:

```
use Framework\Database\Connection\Connection;

class CreateJobsTable
{
    public function migrate(Connection $connection)
    {
        $table = $connection->createTable('jobs');
        $table->id('id');
        $table->text('closure');
        $table->text('params');
        $table->int('attempts')->default(0);
        $table->bool('is_complete')->default(false);
        $table->execute();
    }
}
```

This is from database/migrations/010_CreateJobsTable.php.

We'll see what goes in each of these fields in a little bit. Before we do, though, there's a problem to solve, following on from provider changes I made.

The migrate command was one of the places where we were manually creating a new connection. We could switch out all of that manual work with a call to app('database'), but the way we've set up the App class means none of the providers are loaded before we try and dispatch a route.

We should break these steps up, so that the tests and command.php are able to use all the dependencies the providers configure for us, without needing to dispatch a route:

```
public function prepare(): static
{
    $basePath = $this->resolve('paths.base');

    $this->configure($basePath);
    $this->bindProviders($basePath);
```

```
    return $this;
}

public function run(): Response
{
    return $this->dispatch($this->resolve('paths.base'));
}
```

This is from `framework/App.php`.

Now, we can change the migrate command to use the already configured database connection:

```
protected function execute(InputInterface $input, OutputInterface $output)
{
    $current = getcwd();
    $pattern = 'database/migrations/*.php';

    $paths = glob("{$current}/{$pattern}");

    if (count($paths) < 1) {
        $this->writeln('No migrations found');
        return Command::SUCCESS;
    }

    // $connection = $this->connection();
    $connection = app('database');

    if ($input->getOption('fresh')) {
        $output->writeln('Dropping existing database tables');

        $connection->dropTables();

        // $connection = $this->connection();
        $connection = app('database');
    }

    // ...rest of the migrate code
}
```

```
// private function connection(): Connection
// {
//     $factory = new Factory();

//     $factory->addConnector('mysql', function($config) {
//         return new MysqlConnection($config);
//     });

//     $factory->addConnector('sqlite', function($config) {
//         return new SqliteConnection($config);
//     });

//     $config = require getcwd() . '/config/database.php';

//     return $factory->connect($config[$config['default']]);
// }
```

This is from `framework/Database/Command/MigrateCommand.php`.

Now we need a set of classes we can use, to put jobs into this table and get them out again. Because we want to "store" the closure for later execution, we need a way to serialize it. Closures aren't usually allowed to be serialized, but there are a few lower-level libraries that have been made to enable this. Let's install one of them:

```
composer require opis/closure
```

Serializing closures is a bit magical. There's nothing preventing us from sending string class and method names, so that the methods can be called without serialization. It would be simpler to do so, but I thought this magic would be interesting to demonstrate.

Next, we need to set up the usual provider/manager/driver system, so our framework will be able to support multiple methods of storage and retrieval of these closures:

```
namespace Framework\Provider;

use Framework\Queue\Factory;
use Framework\Queue\Driver\DatabaseDriver;
```

```php
use Framework\Support\DriverProvider;
use Framework\Support\DriverFactory;

class QueueProvider extends DriverProvider
{
    protected function name(): string
    {
        return 'queue';
    }

    protected function factory(): DriverFactory
    {
        return new Factory();
    }

    protected function drivers(): array
    {
        return [
            'database' => function($config) {
                return new DatabaseDriver($config);
            },
        ];
    }
}
```

This is from `framework/Provider/QueueProvider.php`.

This provider depends on a factory and a database driver. The factory is the same as many of our other factories:

```php
namespace Framework\Queue;

use Closure;
use Framework\Queue\Driver\Driver;
use Framework\Queue\Exception\DriverException;
use Framework\Support\DriverFactory;
```

```php
class Factory implements DriverFactory
{
    protected array $drivers;

    public function addDriver(string $alias, Closure $driver): static
    {
        $this->drivers[$alias] = $driver;
        return $this;
    }

    public function connect(array $config): Driver
    {
        if (!isset($config['type'])) {
            throw new DriverException('type is not defined');
        }

        $type = $config['type'];

        if (isset($this->drivers[$type])) {
            return $this->drivers[$type]($config);
        }

        throw new DriverException('unrecognised type');
    }
}
```

This is from framework/Queue/Factory.php.

Each driver needs a couple methods:

1. A push method to push a single task onto the queue

2. A shift method to pull a single task off of the queue

```php
namespace Framework\Queue\Driver;

use Closure;
use Framework\Queue\Job;
```

```
interface Driver
{
    public function push(Closure $closure, ...$params): int;
    public function shift(): ?Job;
}
```

This is from `framework/Queue/Driver/Driver.php`.

The database driver is where the fun happens! We can start off with a shell that implements this interface:

```
namespace Framework\Queue\Driver;

use Closure;
use Framework\Queue\Job;

class DatabaseDriver implements Driver
{
    public function push(Closure $closure, ...$params): int
    {
        // TODO
    }

    public function shift(): ?Job
    {
        // TODO
    }
}
```

This is from `framework/Queue/Driver/DatabaseDriver.php`.

Let's also make a database model, for storing and retrieving the closure and params:

```
namespace Framework\Queue;

use Framework\Database\Model;

class Job extends Model
```

```
{
    public function getTable(): string
    {
        return config('queue.database.table');
    }
}
```

This is from `framework/Queue/Driver/DatabaseQueue.php`.

Oh! We should populate the queue configuration file with this variable:

```
return [
    'default' => 'database',
    'database' => [
        'type' => 'database',
        'table' => 'jobs',
        'attempts' => 3,
    ],
];
```

This is from `config/queue.php`.

This table name should match the name of the table we created in our migration. If you changed it, then don't forget to change it here too.

Using this model and the library we installed earlier, we can serialize the closure and parameters and store them in the database:

```
use Opis\Closure\SerializableClosure;

// ...

public function push(Closure $closure, ...$params): int
{
    $wrapper = new SerializableClosure($closure);

    $job = new Job();
    $job->closure = serialize($wrapper);
```

```
    $job->params = serialize($params);
    $job->attempts = 0;
    $job->save();

    return $job->id;
}
```

This is from `framework/Queue/Driver/DatabaseQueue.php`.

Usually, when you pass a closure to `serialize`, you will see an error. The Opis Closure `SerializableClosure` acts as a wrapper for closures and uses reflection to transform them into something that can be stored as text.

The parameters that we pass to a job are limited to types that can be serialized, without special handling. We can't, for instance, pass `Model` instances or unwrapped closures as parameters.

The corresponding `shift` method should pull a single job out of the jobs table, so that it can be attempted:

```
public function shift(): ?Job
{
    $attempts = config('queue.database.attempts');

    return Job::where('attempts', '<', $attempts)
        ->where('is_complete', false)
        ->first();
}
```

This is from `framework/Queue/Driver/DatabaseQueue.php`.

At this point, there are a couple more things we need to make for this to all work well. The first is that we need a terminal command with which to "process" queued jobs. The second is adding the helpers to the Job model that makes it easier to run, but we'll get to that shortly...

Here's what the terminal command could look like:

```
namespace Framework\Queue\Command;

use Symfony\Component\Console\Command\Command;
use Symfony\Component\Console\Input\InputArgument;
use Symfony\Component\Console\Input\InputInterface;
use Symfony\Component\Console\Input\InputOption;
use Symfony\Component\Console\Output\OutputInterface;
use Exception;

class WorkCommand extends Command
{
    protected static $defaultName = 'queue:work';

    protected function configure()
    {
        $this
            ->setDescription('Runs tasks that have been queued')
            ->setHelp('This command waits for and runs queued jobs');
    }

    protected function execute(InputInterface $input, OutputInterface
    $output)
    {
        $output->writeln('<info>Waiting for jobs.</info>');

        while(true) {
            if ($job = app('queue')->shift()) {
                try {
                    $job->run();

                    $output->writeln("<info>Completed {$job->id}</info>");

                    $job->is_complete = true;
                    $job->save();

                    sleep(1);
                }
```

```
        catch (Exception $e) {
            $message = $e->getMessage();
            $output->writeln("<error>{$message}</error>");

            $job->attempts = $job->attempts + 1;
            $job->save();
        }
    }
  }
 }
}
```

This is from `framework/Queue/Command/WorkCommand.php`.

This terminal command is meant to run continuously while it waits for new jobs to be added to the queue. Notice how it doesn't know a thing about the database, aside from the form of the job being a model.

We could, perhaps, take this a step further and make a form of the `Job` object that doesn't need to be represented as a database model. Alternatively, we could explore the idea of "virtual" models – objects that have the familiar model methods but are stored only in memory. Something akin to Sushi...

As an alternative approach, we could use the Repository Pattern. This would give us an in-memory representation of a data object, without needing to store it in the database. It's a very different design to Active Record, though.

Notice how we expect a `run` method on the Job model:

```
public function run(): mixed
{
    $closure = unserialize($this->closure);
    $params = unserialize($this->params);

    return $closure(...$params);
}
```

This is from `framework/Queue/Job.php`.

Once we've added the work command to `app/comands.php`, then we should be able to add and process queued jobs!

Be careful when trying to unserialize data from an unknown or potentially faulty source. It's possible to alter a serialized string such that arbitrary code can be injected and executed. In other words, do not unserialize user-submitted data.

Even when you trust the source of a serialized string, it can be corrupted via complexity. Always try to serialize to and from a clearly defined and simple specification. Something like JSON is very easy to verify and interpret. It's difficult to make mistakes when encoding primitive values in JSON.

```
app('queue')->push(
    fn($name) => print "Hello {$name}" . PHP_EOL, "Chris"
);

return view('home', [
    'products' => $productsWithRoutes,
]);
```

```
composer serve                                          clear; php command.php queue work

Waiting for jobs.
Hello Chris
Completed 11
```

Running queued jobs

Logging

One of the problems that arise from queueing tasks is that it's more difficult to know when something fails or succeeds, because all of that happens away from the request/response cycle. It's ok if you're running the queue:work command on your computer, but what about when it's running on a remote server?

A potential solution is to introduce a way to log failure and successes during the processing of background tasks.

Logging is another of those problems that is possible to do ourselves, but not really worth the focus of implementing it from the ground up. There are already fantastic open standards for how logging libraries can work, in PHP, like PSR-3.

On top of this, there are libraries that have implemented PSR-3, like Monolog (from the creators of Composer).

Let's build our logging library on top of Monolog:

```
composer require monolog/monolog
```

As usual, we need to create the provider + factory + driver + config combo, starting with the provider:

```
namespace Framework\Provider;

use Framework\Logging\Factory;
use Framework\Logging\Driver\StreamDriver;
use Framework\Support\DriverProvider;
use Framework\Support\DriverFactory;

class LoggingProvider extends DriverProvider
{
    protected function name(): string
    {
        return 'logging';
    }

    protected function factory(): DriverFactory
    {
        return new Factory();
    }
```

```
protected function drivers(): array
{
    return [
        'stream' => function($config) {
            return new StreamDriver($config);
        },
    ];
}
}
```

This is from `framework/Provider/LoggingProvider.php`.

We're starting with a `StreamDriver` (which will write log files to the filesystem). I won't bore you with the factory implementation – as it's almost exactly the same as the others we've made.

You can find the logging factory at `framework/Logging/Factory.php`.

Let's skip ahead to the driver interface:

```
namespace Framework\Logging\Driver;

interface Driver
{
    public function info(string $message): static;
    public function warning(string $message): static;
    public function error(string $message): static;
}
```

This is from `framework/Logging/Driver/Driver.php`.

This is only a subset of what PSR-3 and Monolog support, but they're the most common types of log messages. Feel free to add more methods, if you need them...

Finally, the configuration file and StreamDriver:

```
return [
    'default' => 'stream',
    'stream' => [
        'type' => 'stream',
        'path' => __DIR__ . '/../storage/app.log',
        'name' => 'App',
        'minimum' => \Monolog\Logger::DEBUG,
    ],
];
```

This is from config/logging.php.

```
namespace Framework\Logging\Driver;

use Monolog\Logger;
use Monolog\Handler\StreamHandler;

class StreamDriver implements Driver
{
    private array $config;
    private Logger $logger;

    public function __construct(array $config)
    {
        $this->config = $config;
    }

    public function info(string $message): static
    {
        $this->logger()->info($message);
        return $this;
    }
```

```php
    private function logger()
    {
        if (!isset($this->logger)) {
            $this->logger = new Logger($this->config['name']);
            $this->logger->pushHandler(new StreamHandler($this-
            >config['path'], $this->config['minimum']));
        }

        return $this->logger;
    }

    public function warning(string $message): static
    {
        $this->logger()->warning($message);
        return $this;
    }

    public function error(string $message): static
    {
        $this->logger()->error($message);
        return $this;
    }
}
```

This is from `framework/Logging/Driver/LoggingDriver.php`.

StreamDriver is a decorator around Monolog's StreamHandler class. It handles the Monolog setup, populating it with configuration variables we've defined in `config/logging.php`.

Don't forget to add the `LoggingProvider` class to `config/providers.php`, or the next bit of code won't work.

We can now log failures and successes from anywhere in our application:

```
app('queue')->push(
    fn($name) => app('logging')->info("Hello {$name}"),
    'Chris',
);

app('logging')->info('Send a task into the background');
```

I recommend logging exhaustively inside background tasks, as it will help surface bugs in your code and highlight background processing problems before they start to affect your customers.

Email

The final library we'll work on is one to send emails. There are a couple different practical ways to send email:

1.   Using a system service to send email, which runs alongside the web server

2.   Sending mail through a third-party API

I know, from personal experience, how difficult it is to set up a reliable mail server. There's so much going on in the world of email validation and security that your emails are likely to land in spam folders unless you're an expert in configuration.

By contrast, there are plenty of affordable and expertly configured third-party email APIs to choose from. The process is usually to call an API with a destination email address and email content:

```
curl -X POST
    https://mandrillapp.com/api/1.0/messages/send
    -H "Accept: application/json"
    -H "Content-Type: application/json"
    -d '{
            "key":"[API KEY]"
            "message": {
                "html": "<h1>Welcome to our website</h1>...",
                "text": "Welcome to our website...",
```

```
            "subject": "Registration Complete",
            "to": ["customer@domain.com"]
        }
    }'
```

This is from the Mandrill docs.

We could replicate this, in PHP, but Mailchimp has created a PHP library to speed the process up. This is what it looks like to request the same mail be sent in PHP:

```
$client = new MailchimpTransactional\ApiClient();
$client->setApiKey('[API KEY]');

$client->messages->send([
    'message' => [
        'html' => '<h1>Welcome to our website</h1>...',
        'text' => 'Welcome to our website...',
        'subject' => 'Registration Complete',
        'to' => ['customer@domain.com'],
    ]
]);
```

Postmark has a similar sort of API, which you can also call to send an email:

```
curl -X POST
    "https://api.postmarkapp.com/email"
    -H "Accept: application/json"
    -H "Content-Type: application/json"
    -H "X-Postmark-Server-Token: [API KEY]"
    -d '{
        "From": "sender@domain.com",
        "To": "customer@domain.com",
        "Subject": "Registration Complete",
        "TextBody": "Welcome to our website...",
        "HtmlBody": "<h1>Welcome to our website</h1>...",
    }'
```

This is from the Postmark docs.

Unsurprisingly, Postmark also has a PHP library we can use, to send a similar email:

```php
$client = new Postmark\PostmarkClient('[API KEY]');

$client->sendEmail(
    '[SENDER SIGNATURE]',
    'customer@domain.com',
    'Registration Complete',
    '<h1>Welcome to our website</h1>...',
    'Welcome to our website...'
);
```

There are also email-sending abstractions (similar to what Flysystem does for filesystem abstraction), like SwiftMailer. Let's follow our earlier strategy: which is to build on top of SwiftMailer, but with an API that we prefer. First, we need to install SwiftMailer:

```
composer require swiftmailer/swiftmailer
```

Turns out Postmark also has a SwiftMailer plugin:

```
composer require wildbit/swiftmailer-postmark
```

Next, let's make the provider + factory + driver + configuration combo:

```php
namespace Framework\Provider;

use Framework\Email\Factory;
use Framework\Email\Driver\PostmarkDriver;
use Framework\Support\DriverProvider;
use Framework\Support\DriverFactory;

class EmailProvider extends DriverProvider
{
    protected function name(): string
    {
        return 'email';
    }
}
```

```php
    protected function factory(): DriverFactory
    {
        return new Factory();
    }

    protected function drivers(): array
    {
        return [
            'postmark' => function($config) {
                return new PostmarkDriver($config);
            },
        ];
    }
}
```

This is from framework/Provider/EmailProvider.php.

Check out framework/Email/Factory.php to see how the factory looks. It's the same as the others we've made. The driver includes a bunch of chainable methods, similar to what we did with the QueryBuilder:

```php
namespace Framework\Email\Driver;

interface Driver
{
    public function to(string $to): static;
    public function subject(string $subject): static;
    public function text(string $text): static;
    public function html(string $html): static;
    public function send(): void;
}
```

This is from framework/Email/Driver/Driver.php.

The implementation of this interface works similarly to what we did with the logging driver we implemented, but with a bit more validation:

```php
namespace Framework\Email\Driver;

use Framework\Email\Exception\CompositionException;
use Postmark\Transport;
use Swift_Mailer;
use Swift_Message;

class PostmarkDriver implements Driver
{
    private array $config;
    private Swift_Mailer $mailer;
    private string $to;
    private string $subject;
    private string $text;
    private string $html;

    public function __construct(array $config)
    {
        $this->config = $config;
    }

    public function to(string $to): static
    {
        $this->to = $to;
        return $this;
    }

    public function subject(string $subject): static
    {
        $this->subject = $subject;
        return $this;
    }
}
```

```php
public function text(string $text): static
{
    $this->text = $text;
    return $this;
}

public function html(string $html): static
{
    $this->html = $html;
    return $this;
}

public function send(): void
{
    if (!isset($this->to)) {
        throw new CompositionException('to required');
    }

    if (!isset($this->text) && !isset($this->html)) {
        throw new CompositionException('text or email required');
    }

    $fromName = $this->config['from']['name'];
    $fromEmail = $this->config['from']['email'];

    $subject = $this->subject ?? "Message from {$fromName}";

    $message = (new Swift_Message($subject))
        ->setFrom([$fromEmail => $fromName])
        ->setTo([$this->to]);

    if (isset($this->text) && !isset($this->html)) {
        $message->setBody($this->text, 'text/plain');
    }

    if (!isset($this->text) && isset($this->html)) {
        $message->setBody($this->html, 'text/html');
    }
```

```
        if (isset($this->text, $this->html)) {
            $message
                ->setBody($this->html, 'text/html')
                ->addPart($this->text, 'text/plain');
        }

        $this->mailer()->send($message);
    }

    private function mailer()
    {
        if (!isset($this->mailer)) {
            $transport = new Transport($this->config['token']);
            $this->mailer = new Swift_Mailer($transport);
        }

        return $this->mailer;
    }
}
```

This is from `framework/Email/Driver/PostmarkDriver.php`.

We could probably do more validation to make sure that the format of the $config array is one that we expect, but I'll leave that as an exercise for you. Here's what the ideal configuration file looks like:

```
return [
    'default' => 'postmark',
    'postmark' => [
        'type' => 'postmark',
        'token' => env('EMAIL_TOKEN'),
        'from' => [
            'name' => env('EMAIL_FROM_NAME'),
            'email' => env('EMAIL_FROM_EMAIL'),
        ],
    ]
];
```

This is from `config/email.php`.

All this is to say – once we have added `EmailProvider` to `config/providers.php` – we should be able to send emails easily:

```
app('queue')->push(
    fn($name) => app('email')
        ->to('cgpitt@gmail.com')
        ->text("Hello {$name}")
        ->send(),
    'Chris',
);
```

In this example, I'm sending email inside a queued task. Sending email is usually a slow process, so it's best to do that sort of thing outside of the HTTP request/response cycle.

Caveats

There are many things we could spend even more time attempting. Here are some you might be interested in trying:

1. We've only set up one driver for each of these libraries. Imagine a queue driver that uses Redis or Amazon SQS to store messages or a Slack logging driver.

2. We're making assumptions about many of the configuration file structures. We can't always trust that developers will follow the docs, so we should help them discover when the configuration format is invalid.

3. Popular frameworks like to move driver-based dependencies into suggested dependencies, and they document this approach. Usually, when you want to send emails in Laravel, you need to also install vendor-specific libraries like `wildbit/swiftmailer-postmark`. This is a good pattern, because it means developers won't automatically install dependencies for drivers they don't use.

4. Instead of supporting just one exception handler, we could support a list of many, with the first handler to return a response becoming the "winner."

Summary

This was the final code chapter. We've learned so much about structuring framework code and building up a solid set of libraries to use.

Take some time to look back on the code you've written and the lessons you've learned. I'll start the next chapter talking about some final changes I want to make to the framework and application.

CHAPTER 12

Publishing Your Code

It's time to talk about what happens after our framework is made. Writing code is just the beginning. The hard part is getting people to use it and keeping it fresh and useful.

I think it would help to frame this part of things by talking about what I would still like to do to our framework and example application before I'd be happy putting it out into the world...

Finishing Touches

Every popular framework has a starter kit. These are the kinds of projects you can copy, clone, or otherwise install, in order to see how the code works. These starter kits serve as a kickoff point for new applications. They should be helpful and easy to understand.

With that in mind, here are some things I'd like to add before releasing it to the world.

#1: Helpful Home Page

Making the home page helpful. The first page a user sees should reassure them that things are set up correctly, for them to be able to start developing. There should be links to documentation and other resources they might find useful (like hosting and debugging options).

© Christopher Pitt 2021
C. Pitt, *Pro PHP 8 MVC*, https://doi.org/10.1007/978-1-4842-6957-2_12

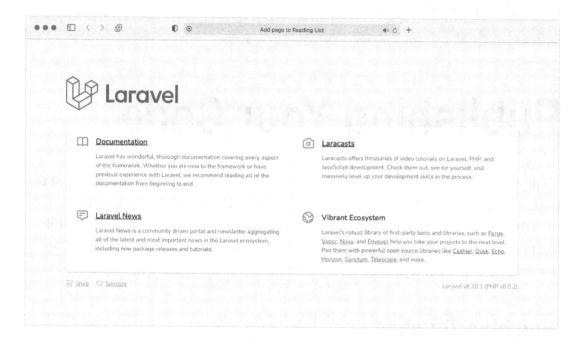

Laravel's helpful home page

This is the first thing you see when you start Laravel's development server. There are only three commands you need in order to see this:

```
composer create-project laravel/laravel my-new-project
cd my-new-project
php artisan serve
```

Starting with a new framework can be a daunting task, so this makes a huge difference. There's no required configuration to "get things going." If you want to start using models (or other database functionality), then you need to set up a database.

Perhaps this could be a little easier by configuring SQLite by default. Then new users wouldn't need to configure anything to be able to use 80% of the framework's functionality.

#2: More Examples of Functionality

We've built so much functionality, but very little of it is demonstrated in the example application. There are some small examples of working with the session and cache. Not much else.

Even if the examples were commented out, it would still be useful to show the appropriate time and manner in which to do common things. We could show how to send emails or do something in a queue or how to put files in a remote filesystem.

This is where tutorials and good documentation do a lot of heavy lifting. Speaking of which...

#3: Good Documentation

Good documentation (or lack thereof) is one of the first and biggest gripes other developers will have with your framework. They want to see how the framework can be used, how it can be configured, where it is supported, and what its limitations are.

There's a huge spectrum your documentation can be on. Laravel is concise and focused on key parts of functionality. The Laravel community (and PHP communities in general) is good at filling in the gaps, in the form of written and video tutorials.

Symfony, on the other hand, has extensive documentation that some may find overwhelming in volume and specificity. I have never had a question about how to use a Symfony component that wasn't answered by the documentation.

The key is to give enough information for how you expect the component to be used most commonly and have links to good community resources for specialized use, optimization, and extension.

The first PHP framework I used was CodeIgniter. It's still alive and kicking (at the time of writing), and it was a great influence in my career. Not because it had the best code or biggest community, but because the documentation told me everything I needed to know in order to learn how to use the framework.

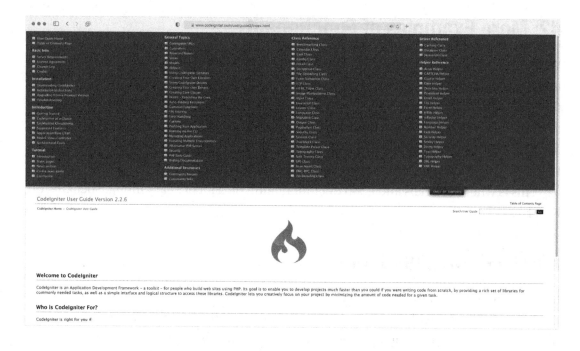

CodeIgniter 2 documentation table of contents

More recent versions have done away with the "introduction," but I guess there are more ways to learn about those topics these days.

#4: Complete Tests

Another big gripe developers have (and rightly so) is when a new framework comes along without a comprehensive and effective test suite. If you want to launch a new framework, make sure you have 90–100% of the functionality it provides covered by automated tests.

You don't need to test third-party code, but you should test the ways you connect to and use it.

Testing can be a tricky subject to learn, even with the right tools, but it's not something you want to cut corners with. Take a course or read a good book on the subject:

- Test-Driven Laravel – Adam Wathan

- PHPUnit: Testing with a Bite – SymfonyCasts

- *The Grumpy Programmer's Guide to Testing PHP Applications* – Chris Hartjes

#5: Make Sure It's What You Want to Do

Building a framework is hard, but it's the easiest part of the journey. Maintaining a framework for years will take up much of your life, if you do it well.

You are far better off taking many smaller parts from the different frameworks and putting them together into something coherent and useful for your purposes.

Or, better yet, learn how to use a popular and well-supported framework yourself. We'll talk more about these in the Afterword.

Using Packagist

Throughout this book, we've installed many libraries using Composer. These libraries are all hosted on a site called Packagist. If you want your framework (or individual libraries) to be installable through Composer, you need to submit it to Packagist.

If you haven't already, create an account. If you're using GitHub to host your code, you may as well use GitHub to log into Packagist.

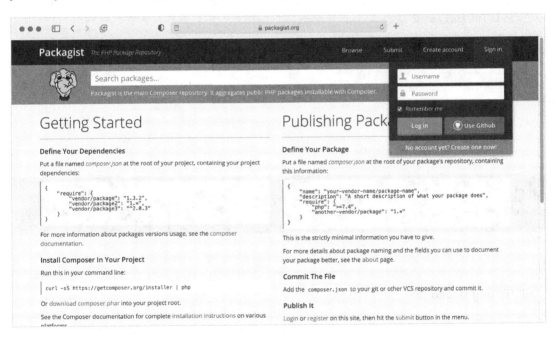

Signing in with GitHub

Your library needs to have a well-defined `composer.json` file. I don't want to go too deeply into the specifics of this, because it's an art all on its own.

If you're at this point and want to know how to publish your own packages, then check out a video course like PHP Package Development. It covers details about the `composer.json` specification, as well as teaching how to properly structure stand-alone Composer packages really well.

The full `composer.json` specification takes quite a bit of time to understand, and you can find it on the Composer documentation site.

Once you've put one together, submit it through Packagist's submission form.

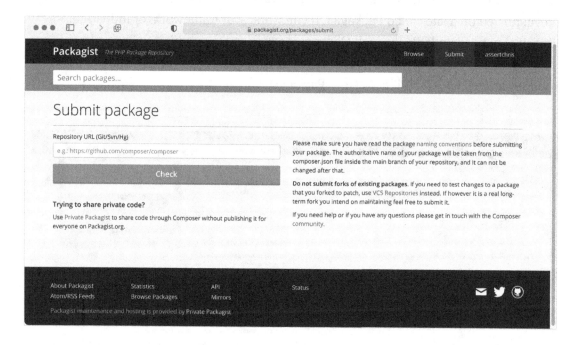

Submitting packages

Then, you (or anybody else) will be able to install your library through a `composer require` terminal command. That's really all there is to it.

Summary

If you remember nothing else about this chapter, let it be this: maintaining a framework is hard work. Building one is a rite of passage and a brilliant way to learn how they work, but it's a big decision to own a framework. It's not an easy task.

Hopefully, this chapter has given you a look into some of the challenges that await and things you should consider. I'll see you in the Afterword of this book.

Wrapping Up

I've had a wonderful time writing this book. It's been a long and sometimes stressful 10 months, but I feel like it's been worth it. If you've read all the way through, then I want to thank you for making that investment of time.

I want to thank Matthias for his stellar review and insight and Apress for the chance to make something better of this book.

So much of what we do, as developers, isn't about the code we write. We begin every bit of important work from a brief and end every bit of important work with a demonstration.

Sometimes the person giving us the brief and receiving the demonstration is ourselves, but so often it's someone else, with a different set of expectations and skills. Someone with a different story.

As a framework developer (and a developer in general), you will best serve yourself and others by listening intently to what they want and learning how to communicate the use and value of your creations.

Until you learn how to be a good communicator, you cannot and will not achieve success in your efforts to make the next big framework.

Maybe you have the skill and determination to make the next Laravel or Symfony. I hope you do. Before you get there, you need to learn how to listen and talk in a way that will make people stick around. You'll need to figure out what your fellow developers need and put their needs (at least in the short term) above your own desires.

Or you could just use this as a learning experience and find a good framework to use at your day job. There's no shame in that. You've made yourself better by learning.

© Christopher Pitt 2021
C. Pitt, *Pro PHP 8 MVC*, https://doi.org/10.1007/978-1-4842-6957-2

Index

© Christopher Pitt 2021
C. Pitt, *Pro PHP 8 MVC*, https://doi.org/10.1007/978-1-4842-6957-2

W, X, Y, Z

Printed in the United States
by Baker & Taylor Publisher Services